To
The Read

Martha Kamirak Blonkey

Gift from:
Polish National alliance, Group 848
5119 TEMPLE Hills Rd. S.E
WASHINGTON D.C 20031

THE MASK OF WARRIORS

The Mask of Warriors

The Siege of Warsaw, September 1939

by

Marta Korwin-Rhodes

LIBRA PUBLISHERS, Inc.

To my husband, Herbert G. E. Rhodes, with gratitude for his support and encouragement

INTRODUCTION

This book is an account of one person's experience in the siege of Warsaw, September 1-30, 1939.[1] It does not give a total picture of the siege, but rather a series of necessarily incomplete sketches showing the role of some individuals in an important historical event.

I was fortunate to have access to the daily records, or diary, of Maltanski Hospital, an emergency military hospital established under the auspices of the Sovereign Order of the Knights of Malta. In that record book, two secretaries noted events hourly throughout the siege, and other staff members recorded some of their experiences. Pasted into the book are messages from defense headquarters, press clippings, photographs, and German leaflets that were dropped on the city.

This document is now in the custody of Prince Olgierd Czartoryski, ambassador to Brazil of the Sovereign Order of the Knights of Malta.

At dawn on September 1, 1939, a German bomb hit Poland —the first blow in the attack that started World War II.

For many days before that, a German fifth column had been harassing the country with that precursor of armed aggression, sabotage.

One form of the sabotage—the removal from circulation of silver and copper coins—had brought Warsaw almost to a standstill. Later it was discovered that German agents, acting on orders from Berlin, had hoarded thousands of zlotys in small change.

Sabotage does not need to be violent to be effective. Can you imagine what happens when suddenly all coinage vanishes from circulation? Not to be able to buy a package of cigarettes or a cup of coffee, to pay carfare or to make a telephone call? Millions of everyday transactions depend on having the right change.

When the shortage of coins was noticeable, people became angry at each other and at the government. Bitter arguments took place in bakeries over loaves of bread, in drug stores over a few aspirin tablets, and in the post office over a stamp. By such simple but cunning sabotage the Germans aroused a people to anger, thus undermining friendships, trust, and respect for government. Moreover, it turned attention away from international tensions.

Whether the Germans achieved their purpose by hoarding coinage before attacking Poland remains a mystery. The first day of bombing, at any rate, relegated the whole matter to insignificance.

On the day before the attack I wandered through the streets of Warsaw in the autumn sunshine. I saw no signs of excitement. Most people felt aware there was a state of diplomatic tension, but believed that it would only be a war of nerves. At night the cafes were noisy and gay with life and laughter.

Friday, September 1, 1939

At 6:15 A.M. the sirens began sounding; simultaneously we heard German bombers. Without warning Germany had attacked Poland along its whole German border—the terribly long one. We had learned from films about that goose-stepping mass of soldiery, parading before their Führer, longing to prove that they could conquer for him. At Hitler's command the contained build-up of years erupted. Soldiers poured like lava from Germany in the south and East Prussia in the north, cutting Poland into two. On the ground, tanks rolled. The armored Panzer divisions had been carefully designed to end the war in Poland in six days, then to turn westward, conquering all Europe by the end of September.

Squadron after squadron of Goering's Luftwaffe flew deep into Poland and within the first few hours bombed every strategic point. After the airplanes dumped cargoes of bombs, they machine-gunned everything that moved.

At 6:15 that morning I was still awake, having just come home from a very enjoyable dance. I remembered that the previous January, when there were some emergency exercises for civilians in Warsaw, I had received an official notification: that the occupant of apartment number seventeen is designated in case of war to go to the roof of the apartment house when the sirens sounded to act as fire-watcher. In my evening gown I went up to the roof. It was an exciting spectacle—bombers flying in formation, and dog fights between the Luftwaffe and our few planes that had escaped destruction on the ground. Some planes went down, leaving trails of smoke behind; I was certain they were the enemy's and I was pleased.

I could see smoke from whatever was set on fire and wondered what had been hit. This spectacle lasted for about an hour, and then everything was as quiet as if nothing had happened. I returned to my apartment and turned on the radio.

War was on, there was no doubt about it. News was interrupted again and again by messages in code: "Sector X attention! Attention! It approaches!" followed by "Sector X attention! Attention! It crossed!" This code was rather clear, and the messages went on the whole day, almost without interruption.

Every radio in the country was busy. We were waiting for the most vital news—had our allies, France and England, declared war on Germany?

In compliance with the regulations, I filled the bathtub and all possible containers with water, although I thought it was a silly thing to do.

At noon the sirens sounded again. From my post, as firewatcher on the roof, I looked down on the street below. In spite of all efforts to direct the people to safety, most stood in the open, gazing skyward.

At five P.M. the sirens again sounded. This time the bombing lasted for two hours.

In the evening a few friends came to see me. My cousin, a reserve officer, arrived from the country, north of Vilno. He was to report to his unit in Warsaw the next day. He told us that in his village, the mayor had received orders to distribute mobilization cards to a few specified young men. It had happened that those receiving the cards were his relatives. The other young men of the village had felt insulted that they were not among the chosen few, and had held a meeting. The poor mayor had had nothing to do with the choice; his duty was simply to pass on the envelopes to the addresses. The other men, however, believed he had shown favoritism toward his own friends, and almost expressed their anger in violence.

My cousin told us also that at one railroad station on the way to Warsaw, some young men who had been called were so eager to join their units that they had laid themselves across the rails, forcing the express to stop and pick them up.

The allied governments had constantly enjoined us not to effect a general mobilization, in order "to avoid irritating Germany," and therefore we had been restricted to calling up some reserves secretly. With some bitterness we remembered that though Marshal Pilsudski had been warning us since 1933, of the danger of German aggression, the western countries had preferred to shut their eyes, giving Germany opportunity to rearm.

By that time, the evening of September first, it was known that the whole country had been bombed during the day, that many small towns and villages were already in ruins, and that the planes had dived to machine-gun children in the fields. Photographs in the evening newspapers substantiated what was difficult for us to believe.

Although the population of Germany was more than twice that of Poland, we still believed that if we did mobilize our manpower we would have a chance, as we trusted our courage and the justice of our cause. Perhaps it would have been so if we had had tanks and an adequate air force instead of horses.

Although war had been brought home to us, although every region in the country had been bombed, and many people had lost their lives and their possessions, it had not yet reached our consciousness that the nature of war had changed. The old concept of wars fought between armies, preferably on enemy territory, with civilians suffering some privation, or loss of a dear one, but otherwise remote from direct action—this antique heritage still was very much in our minds. We still believed that someone who was not drafted could take the war or leave it. We did not realize that day, or in the next few days, that in modern war there are no choices; everyone participates, and it is everyone's responsibility.

Saturday, September 2, 1939

At daybreak, we had two hours of bombing. Attending to my duties on the roof, I was making some decisions. Recently I had become recognized as a concert pianist. I had already played in Europe, the Near East, and the United States. Only the year before I had made a tour with forty-eight recitals. That autumn a concert tour through Asia and North America had been planned for me, which would take me around the world for the first time. It was to start in October, and I was ready. My physical condition was excellent; my wardrobe had been designed in Paris. However, what was most important, I felt that my program carried a message. All I had to do, I believed, was to drive away from danger, have a little vacation on the Black Sea, and proceed with the tour. Many years of work and discipline had been invested in preparing for the tour, so I did not want to give it up.

Why not leave after the raid was over, I asked myself, before the noon bombing comes? As a concert pianist, I could do much for my country. Paderewski, Rubinstein— they carried a message through their music. I could do the same. But what message could I carry if I left Warsaw now? Would it be possible to live in peace with myself, knowing that I had abandoned my country in need?

As I sat on a box of sand on the roof, a fire extinguisher in my hands, watching a battle in the sky and huge clouds of black smoke across the Vistula River, a struggle went on between my most important values. When the "all clear" sounded, I returned to my apartment. It is sad to wipe out a future. I was so sorry for myself that nothing else in the world mattered to me, and I shed a few tears at the funeral of my concert career.

Soon after nine A.M. I presented myself to the Red Cross to volunteer my services. The Red Cross had not yet adjusted to the new type of warfare. I was most cordially received, but there was not a thing they thought I could do—perhaps later, some concerts to raise money. . . . It was very frustrating.

At lunch, after the noon bombing, I met Princess Isabelle Radziwill, who invited me to help her to organize a Malta Corps to care for the wounded. Very willingly I accepted. During World War I, Isabelle had had a distinguished record. The experience gained had added to her energy, initiative, and good will. Nothing ever seemed to be too difficult for her—her ideas were always on a large scale. All this, backed by her good looks, her historic name, and her large fortune, made for success in any enterprise she undertook.

Isabelle was *Soeur en Chef de L'Ordre Souverin de Malte* in Poland—head of the staff that would work in Poland under the auspices of the Knights of Malta.[2]

In preparation for the possibility of war, the Order of Malta had divided the country into regions, with a delegate in charge of the organization of each region. The delegate for Warsaw was Dominik Lempicki, Knight of Honor and Devotion. The head of the Knights of Malta in Poland was Prince Janusz Radziwill, Isabelle's cousin.

I learned that arrangements had been made for the Order's close cooperation with both the military authorities and the Red Cross. Plans were based on World War I experience.

It was foreseen by Polish authorities that the two German armies, attacking from East Prussia and from Germany, would try to meet and thus cut off the western part of Poland. It was expected that our regular army would hold the invader at that line until our own manpower was mobilized, and until our allies joined us in our defense. (Our alliance with Great

Britain and France bound those countries, in case one of the three allies was attacked, to enter the war.)

It was the second day of the war and neither of our allies had moved.

We had also an alliance with Romania; in case either of the two countries was attacked the other army was to join automatically in defense activities, and the Polish commander-in-chief was to take command over both armies. We did not know what was happening to this alliance. We, the ordinary people, had no reason to think that Romania would find it profitable to violate this agreement and arrest our commander-in-chief and his staff when they crossed the Romanian frontier. However, that is what happened, though we in Warsaw did not know of it until later.

The Order's preparations for helping wounded soldiers were impressive. Over 100 homes in the eastern part of the country, "away from the danger of war," had been offered for use as hospitals.

In the afternoon of the second day of the war, the military authorities asked Isabelle to set up a hospital immediately in Lublin. We wondered if the University of Lublin would be still available.

Before she departed, we discussed the general scheme, and decided that we must without delay build up our own personnel by organizing a course of training for auxiliary nurses. To train nurses we needed permission from the Red Cross. I must admit that it was pleasurable to return to the place where my services had been turned down a few hours earlier to negotiate on so important a matter as training staffs for 100 hospitals and two hospital trains. After the Red Cross gave its sanction, I was put in charge of the training for the duration of the war, with a carte blanche for ways and means. An announcement was placed in the newspapers that candidates for auxiliary nursing could now enroll at our office, and that classes would start on the following Tuesday, September fifth. At this stage we had neither teachers nor classrooms.

Isabelle went to Lublin, and I began to scout for lecturers. Training for auxiliary nurses consisted of ninety hours of lectures, followed by an examination, and then 300 hours of hospital work. I felt it was important to combine class teaching with practical experience, and wondered whether it was possible to squeeze the course into a month. That would mean thirteen hours a day for thirty days. This did not seem possible, as some additional homework is always necessary. However, I felt that, in a month, we might take up all the theory, with at least some practical experience.

Fifth columnists had hung metallic discs on trees throughout the country. These discs, twinkling in the sun, could be seen from a great altitude, and pointed out the right way to enemy planes so that they would not waste time searching for their targets.

Sunday, September 3, 1939

Early in the morning the citizens of Warsaw were called upon over the radio to dig trenches to shelter people from bombing and machine-gunning. As they dug they were machine-gunned from the air, but they continued with the work.

At noon loudspeakers installed in the streets announced that Great Britain had declared war on Germany. It was an electrifying moment! It seemed as if the whole population dashed into the streets. Warsaw overflowed with joy. People were laughing and crying. Crowds thronged the streets leading to the British Embassy. Loudspeakers urged us to avoid crowds and to take shelter immediately, as bombers were overhead. But the people pressed on, heedless of death from the air. The people could not remain in one place; a restless, feverish, hectic elation drove them on.

A new feature of modern war appeared—the refugee. Motor cars crammed with people sped toward the city. One could not buy gasoline any more that day, so many cars were left abandoned. Horse carts packed with men, women, and children, tired and wan, trundled laboriously along; bicycles, with old and young bent down with bundles on their backs, and innumerable parcels hanging from the handlebars, threaded their ways through both the quiet and the busy streets, wandering aimlessly. People had fled from their homes and had been bombed and machine-gunned on the roads. They had fled to the "safety" of the capital of the country, but only found more bombers over Warsaw. The people of Warsaw opened their homes to those desperate refugees and shared their already scarce food with them.

From all parts of the country came men who had not been called to the army, or who were under or over military age. They wanted to force the authorities to let them enlist. They did not want to be spectators.

In the late afternoon, when we learned that France had declared war on Germany, enthusiastic demonstrations took place before the French Embassy.

Isabelle Radziwill returned from Lublin in the evening, reporting that Lublin had suffered greatly from bombing, and that all the buildings in the city that were suitable for hospitals had been commandeered by the military. She had been asked by the military authorities to go to Brzesc and Pinsk to establish hospitals, and she planned to leave the next day.

We talked about the course for auxiliary nurses. A lecture room to accommodate the crowd we expected had been made available. Lecturers were lined up—not an easy matter, because doctors below the age of fifty were being drafted and many had to report to their assignments soon, in the eastern and northeastern parts of the country.

Late at night, as I walked home, a red rocket shot upward in the darkness. I saw nobody; I heard nothing. I felt uneasy, as if in the presence of a ghost. What fiend had fired it? What message did it convey?

Monday, September 4, 1939

Isabelle had expected to be away for at least two weeks, if she could manage to find some buildings for hospital use in Brzesc and Pinsk. She asked me whether my brother Stas[3] could go with her. Stas, who was in the Foreign Office, felt very badly about having been exempted from military service. He had tried unsuccessfully to pull strings in order to be called. I telephoned him and he was very pleased to be asked to go and be useful. They left shortly before noon.

Rumors began to circulate that Warsaw would be occupied by the enemy and that the city was being evacuated.

The registration for auxiliary nurses was very heavy, but we had already had a few withdrawals because of the rumored evacuation. Courses were scheduled to begin the next day, but we had little idea how many students would attend. Before evening I got in touch with some of the instructors; I found that some of them had already left the city or were planning to leave the next day. That meant we were faced with the difficult task of finding replacements. We also had to find replacements for a few of our volunteers who had left the city.

We were bombed regularly three times daily, for two or three hours at a time. We became used to the routine, and could relax when the daily raids were over.

Sometimes leaflets fell from the sky, telling us a few things about ourselves, our leaders, and our allies.

That day, Praga, the district of Warsaw on the east side of the Vistula, was the enemy target. Formations of bombers unloaded sticks of high explosives. The rattle of the machine-guns of our fighters was distinctly heard. I saw three planes crash in flames. Praga was covered with a pall of terrible black smoke.

The newspapers came out as usual that evening, with nothing changed in the advertisements or in the style of reporting. They continued to print pictures of burning buildings and reports of personal impressions and experiences. We knew that many people had been slaughtered, and that many had been made destitute. The papers described how stoutly the flames were fought, and what great dangers were being risked. There were many stores of heroic efforts to save friends from burning houses. (Two weeks later, there were no more newspapers.) The fires burned where they would and what they would. There is no possibility of fighting such vast conflagrations; there was neither manpower nor water. In the fire and smoke the people lived, defended themselves, and died.

In the afternoon my sister arrived. Her husband[4] had joined his regiment on September 1. They lived near Poznan, west of Warsaw, which was considered a vulnerable city. Everyone thought it would be the first to be attacked in the case of war, and accordingly my sister planned to take her two small children and go to our brother Andrew's estate, which was considered safe. It was northeast of Warsaw, almost on the Soviet border, away from the expected front. They had had an exhausting journey from the west and needed rest before traveling any further. As Isabelle Radziwill had left her house at my disposal, I took advantage of her courtesy and installed my sister and her children there in relative safety.

The house was in the embassy district and so far had been spared by the bombing. And it had a bomb shelter in the garden.

Another network of sabotage, organized to break the people's morale, was then revealed. In the region of Poznan, fifth columnists delivered false telegrams in the rural areas, telling families that a soldier or civilian relative had been killed. My sister told me that our friends the Brzeskis had ended their lives when they were informed by a fase telegram that their children, who had been evacuated from the city, had been killed.

In the evening it was announced that Warsaw would have to defend itself to try and stop the advance of the enemy. The people, that is, those who were not then on defense duty, took to their spades again to erect barricades. We were aware that the defense lines had crumbled, but did not know how long it would be before the enemy attacked the capital. Some expected it to be in a few hours, others, a week. Warsaw was flat, and had no natural defenses. The Vistula cut the city into two parts, which made things more difficult for us.

Tuesday, September 5, 1939

My hope for a restful night was shattered by my brother Stas, who burst into my room at four A.M. like a thunderstorm. He said I had made a coward and a deserter of him; that it was only when he arrived with Isabelle at Brzesc that he was informed of the immediate necessity of Warsaw's defending itself. There was no longer any regular transportation between Brzesc and the capital. If he had not found out that a railroad engine was going back to Warsaw, and volunteered to help deliver it to its destination, he would have had to walk 250 miles. When he accepted the fact that I had not yet known about plans for the defense of Warsaw when I had asked him to go to Brzesc, his anger disappeared, and he described his exciting experiences on his return from Brzesc. Railroad centers had been bombed on September 1 and continued to be daily targets. The railroad tracks were twisted and torn, and his engine encountered many obstacles. It was an unusual journey that I felt he had greatly enjoyed.

About seven in the morning I was on my way to the Malta Corps office, and for the first time I saw dive bombing. It was as if silver butterflies in formation came noiselessly down out of the transparent and pale daytime moon. Although they were enemies, I could not help but admire the masterly hands guiding the craft.

There was by then hardly any means of transportation. Buses had been commandeered to convey documents to safer places; besides, gasoline was terribly scarce. I saw the country's gold being taken out of the Treasury vaults and loaded by anyone who could give a hand into several city buses, which were then driven away, escorted by a handful of men who were not even civil servants.[5]

Many streetcars had been converted into barricades. There was still, however, considerable traffic. Many people left the city; many others entered it to help in its defense.

Social classes, political affiliations, and age differences seemed to have evaporated; now we were all Poles. Now people realized that this was a different war. It was not just a soldiers' war; it was everyone's.

Announcements and orders were read over the radio. From loudspeakers in the streets one could hear, "Number Sixty Pulawski Avenue is burning," or, "Parachutists have landed in the Lazienki Park, dressed as streetcar conductors," or "Rocket signals were seen in the Saska Kepa residential section." As each message came through, those living in the neighborhood mentioned rushed to the danger point. Orders given from the broadcasting station were carried out immediately.

As for our training course for auxiliary nurses, it was necessary to find replacements for the instructors who were unable to come. In the afternoon Prince Janusz Radziwill came to my office for a conference concerning staff training. We then went to open the course. The attendance was about 200. The students asked that the lectures be concentrated; they were prepared to work day and night, so an examination could be held as soon as possible.[6]

Wednesday, September 6, 1939

Shortly after four A.M. I was walking through the city to call for my sister to take her and her two children to the railroad station. The day before she had been unable to leave Warsaw because trains leaving for the east were packed to capacity, with every standing place taken. For the past two days there had been no taxicabs in Warsaw. Some old horse-driven cabs had reappeared, but it was very difficult to secure their services. My sister had a reservation for the 6:30 A.M. train. I doubted whether the trains would keep prewar schedules and honor reservations. However, my sister needed help, and so I walked at that early hour through almost deserted streets.

On the way I met Count Stephan Zyberg-Plater, better known as Photo Plat, who was a distant relative of my brother-in-law. He was one of the men and women of my generation and social stratum who went into business. Photo-Plat was the name of his successful photographic agency. The agency's specialty was taking pictures related to current events. He had a flair for being at the right place when something unexpected would happen, and taking a unique shot. When I ran into Stephan he too was on his way to help my sister. Since there were no porters, his help was most welcome.[7]

We talked about the raid in the district of Praga across the Vistula the day before. He had been there taking photographs, which appeared in the evening papers. He had seen houses crashing down, covering the roads and pavements with dust and masses of masonry, and burying men, women, and children under the debris. There had been heroic attempts to rescue the wounded and carry out the dead. Many people could have been rescued, but were not, because of the lack of adequate apparatus and equipment. Much of the courageous rescue efforts had been wasted. Stephan felt, however, that it was not so much lack of equipment that had hampered the attempts of the rescuers, but lack of efficient direction. It was not until the Brothers of St. Albert came from their orphanage with the older boys and took command that really successful rescue work became possible.

We took my sister to the station, which we found damaged by bombing. It was packed with troops and with refugees from western Poland. I went to the stationmaster to find out if there was a possibility of my sister's getting a place on a train. "The train may leave at seven o'clock," he said, "but it may not. It is meant for troops only—but there may be two cars for refugees. Do you know that on the lower platform thousands of refugees have been waiting forty-eight hours for a train? Small children in such a throng will certainly be crushed." Then, rather grimly, he added, "One thing at least is certain—the station will be bombed again before seven o'clock." Yes, one could count on it, without fail.

I took my sister back to Isabelle's home and returned home myself. I managed to struggle onto the steps of an overcrowded streetcar. My brain surged with what I had just heard of the bombing of the Praga district. However, amidst the jostling, swaying, and discomfort, I was convinced before reaching my home that we must organize as as we had never done before; we must have first-aid parties, rescue teams, and first-aid posts. We must have them now, at once.

At breakfast I thought it over and telephoned Prince Janusz Radziwill to ask whether he would meet with me as early as he could to consider how to handle the new situation. As it was still very early, I visited the hairdresser to have my hair cut off, as short hair seemed more suitable for present conditions.

On my way to the office a weeping woman stopped me and begged help for her wounded young son, who, with other schoolboys, had been guarding public buildings in Poznan. Her boy had been wounded in the groin by a bomb splinter on the first of September, and the wound had been dressed then, but not since. When the Germans had approached Poznan, she had feared reprisals, as she had heard that the Germans were executing persons who had been involved in action against them. She had put the boy in a cart to bring him to Warsaw; and the journey had taken all this time. During that long and difficult journey the wound had received no attention, and now all her efforts to find a place for him in a hospital had proved futile. What could I do? I felt myself staring into blackness, for I was not even an auxiliary nurse myself, and could think of no one who was. I took their Warsaw address, and told the brave mother to go home and wait until I could send someone to change the dressing. I I assured her that I was taking responsibility for having her son's wound treated.

Then my larger plans changed. For, if already on the sixth day of the bombing there was no room in the hospitals for a boy wounded in course of his duty, I realized we must set up hospitals first and then attend to first-aid posts.

I searched my memory for an acquaintance who was a nurse or an auxiliary nurse, and who might not be fully occupied. After much thinking I remembered Josette Karszo-Siedlewski. She was very rich, and an only daughter. Her days were a round of pleasure—riding, tennis, dinner parties, and dances —presumably not the best training for a career of tireless devo-

tion, day and night, to the suffering wounded. Still, I remembered that during the preceding winter she had attended a
Red Cross course for auxiliary nurses and had made a fine
rating. That had surprised all her friends, because we had
not thought her capable of perseverance and all that such
a course required. She had had no hospital experience that I
was aware of, nor, I thought, had she ever seen a wound,
unless in a picture.

But I was desperate to make a start. I called her up, and
she came immediately, so I placed the boy under her care until
we could take him to the hospital that was still to be founded.

Josette, thinking frantically of what she had learned of
first aid that could apply to this situation, and conscious of
her limitations, yet realizing, as I did, that desperate situations
demanded desperate endeavors, took charge of her first
patient. With such diligence and luck did she care for him,
that she saved the boy's leg, and probably his life.

Later on, when she and I could lift the mask of warriors for
a moment and glance into ourselves as human beings, Josette
confessed that when she had finished attending to the badly
infected wound, and closed the apartment door behind her,
she had been sick, right there on the staircase.

In the meantime Photo-Plat, who was organizing rescue
teams for the Malta Corps, had called at our office. We made
a list for him of equipment we thought might be needed—
ropes, hatchets, shovels, picks, wheelbarrows, stretchers, and
so on. We thought it a great asset for our team that he was
undertaking this very important task, for whatever he undertook he carried out conscientiously and well. We relieved
him of these duties with the rescue team very soon, as we
felt it was more important that he should utilize his skill in
photography and his courage, which enabled him to be in
bombing target areas.

Prince Janusz Radziwill arrived. I shared my observations
with him and told him what I thought we should begin to

do in Warsaw. He informed me that Isabelle would not be able to return, and that as head of the Order of Malta, he was authorizing me to assume immediately the position of *Soeur en Chef de L'Ordre Souverin de Malte*. He said that he trusted my judgment and my leadership, and that he knew I was well known to Warsaw people in all walks of life. We discussed finances in rather theoretical ways—the banks were closed. I felt that we should dedicate ourselves to this work without holding back anything, and "anything" meant any personal vested interests. People who felt the same as we did, who were willing to sacrifice their convenience, their material possessions, and in fact their lives, would join us. I felt we would not have much difficulty in going ahead with any scheme that would meet the needs of this new type of war.

In Poland's value system, when its independence is threatened, the country takes priority over personal needs.

Prince Radziwill stated that he would not be surprised at any sacrifice our people might make for their country. We were joined by his daughter, Countess Potocki, whose husband was secretary to our embassy in Spain. She offered her home for use as a first-aid post. Her house, known as Potocki Palace, was conveniently located on the main artery of the city, Krakowskie Przedmiescie. Our office already occupied the first floor of the Palace.

The delegate of the Order of Malta for the region of Warsaw was Dominik Lempicki, Knight of Honor and Devotion, whom I had known for many years. We had met socially, but for no apparent reason, rarely had we seen eye to eye: often there had been much antipathy. Therefore I was not at all enthusiastic upon learning that we would have to cooperate closely.

Prince Radziwill, Dominik Lempicki, and I discussed the matter of first-aid posts and rescue teams, and the necessity of opening a hospital in Warsaw. We decided to go ahead with the hospital, and operate rescue teams from the hospital.

Our thinking began to adjust to the constant emergencies of the blitzkrieg situation, which meant often abandoning some cherished plan, in which much work and devotion had been invested. We dropped the idea of first-aid posts, for example, mainly because a network of such posts required a competent person in charge of each one, a sound inter-communication system, and means of taking those badly wounded to hospitals. The difficulty I had experienced in efforts to secure instructors for auxiliary nurses' training made it clear that the shortage of medical and nursing personnel soon would become desperate. The telephone exchange was a frequent bombing target; several times already we had been without telephone service for a few hours. Gasoline was requisitioned and the shortage was acute. Those difficulties could be overcome, but the fact that the hospitals were overcrowded on the sixth day of the war made us face the reality of the present situation; with each air raid there were more casualties and less room in hospitals. What would we do with those seriously wounded whom we treated in first-aid posts?

Our most pressing needs were a hospital and rescue teams. We felt that priority should be given to the areas of the city where there were no hospitals. We looked over the map of Warsaw. Warsaw was proud of its hospitals; most had beautiful locations. But from the map it became obvious that several hospitals would find themselves beyond the barricades, and those in the city would not be easily accessible when transportation became more difficult. Hospitals in Warsaw were planned for a peaceful society, but we were at war. The city itself was to become a battlefield; one could only speculate what that would entail.

We agreed on a course of action, leaving much room for flexibility. In this short conference I gained respect for Dominik's quick grasp of problems and situations. As the days wore on, I came to respect him more and more. When in the last days of the siege he was killed on duty, it was a terrible blow to us all. We lost a gallant chief of staff, a most devoted colleague, and a loyal friend.

Prince Radziwill said he and his wife were leaving Warsaw before noon. At his estate, which was in northeast Poland, he was to be host to the President of the Republic. The President was to leave Warsaw that afternoon. We understood that the chief executive of a country, automatically chief of the armed forces, cannot function in a besieged capital. Nevertheless we felt sad, and deep, deep inside we had a sensation of being abandoned.

Prince Radziwill departed and we went to work. We called the radio stations and asked that our need for a suitable building be announced. Within a few minutes the announcement was on the air, and soon we began to receive suggestions and offers. Any building we might have chosen would have been handed over immediately by its owner; sacrifice and willingness to help were boundless.

While we were weighing choices for the hospital I was worrying about who could take charge of the nursing staff, and I was at a loss. There must be someone, I knew, indeed more than one, able and willing to undertake the task. This person should be with us when we finally chose our building. The Red Cross was undergoing a metamorphosis from peacetime slow motion to blitzkrieg requirements. We had to depend upon ourselves for the next few days.

At an earlier time, going through the applications for auxiliary nurses' training, I had come across an applicant with particularly striking qualifications. She had served as a nurse in World War I and had been decorated with the Military Cross. She was a widow, directing her own prosperous business. The reason she had wanted to take our course was to bring herself up to date and to join the Malta Corps. I had felt she had much strength and leadership, and thought of bearing her in mind for some important assignment. I could not, however, remember her name, and I had no access to our records, as they were in another part of the city.

We made tentative choices and it was time to go out to examine buildings, to see which could be most easily adapted to a hospital. But my thoughts kept searching into nothingness for this will-o'-the-wisp nurse, who seemed so close to me, yet ever eluded my sight and reach. Perhaps I shall see her at the lecture tonight, I thought. Perhaps she was working elsewhere. The need for nurses was urgent, for the number of wounded was increasing every hour. Oh, I thought, if I could only find her now! At this point the door opened, and my unknown nurse entered the room. I never discovered what she had wanted then, or why she had come. I told her of our plans and what we expected her to do. She agreed, and, with our new director of nursing, Mrs. Barbara Glinski, Dominik Lempicki and I went out.

It was noon. We walked in Indian file close to the walls, because the enemy bombers were overhead, and splinters of anti-aircraft shells were raining around us. We noticed that our planes were no longer in the air.

We spent two hours looking for a suitable building. Then we deliberated over three: Ostrowki Palace, Resursa Obywatelska Club, and Resursa Kupiecka Club. We were predisposed toward the third one. Our favorable attitude was intensified because, as we neared it, a plane heading in that direction was hit and went down in flames, and when we entered the hall the "All clear" sounded. That made us feel safe.

After deciding on the Resursa Kupiecka Club for a hospital, we separated. Mrs. Glinski remained behind to acquaint herself thoroughly with the building. Dominik undertook the responsibility of requisitioning of the building and establishing a working relationship with the army command of the defence of Warsaw. It fell to me to staff and to equip the hospital.

I returned to the office soon after two o'clock. Our clerical staff had vanished, but Josette was waiting there. She
had brought two sandwiches and a bar of chocolate, which
we shared for lunch. She was very proud of having been
able to change the dressing and attend to the wound of our
first patient, and was thrilled with the news of our plans for
the hospital. I felt that her newly revealed courage, ability
to take responsibility, and spirit of adventure were attributes
needed for the position of my assistant, so I asked her
whether she would like to join the Malta Corps in this
capacity. Then to urgent business. Our clerical department
had been crumbling throughout the morning. When our
volunteer staff had offered their services to help in the war
effort, they did not dream that the reality of the situation
would require working on a battlefield such as Warsaw was
now becoming. After the morning raid, only one typist had
remained at her post, but now she was gone. As neither of
us could type, Josette went to bring the typist back or to
find a replacement.

We needed staff and we needed equipment. I had no illusions that my knowledge of what was needed for a hospital
was other than superficial. It would have been preposterous
for me to specify what was needed, but I felt it would be
appropriate to communicate to the people of Warsaw what
we planned and to ask their help. We would use the newspapers as one means of communication, asking them to print
a concise announcement, and would use the radio for personal communication of current needs.

The communiqué for newspapers was very simple: It
stated that the Sovereign Order of the Knights of Malta was
opening a hospital in Resursa Kupiecka on Senatorska Avenue, and that it needed beds, bedclothes, mattresses, blankets,
pillows, and so forth. We left "and so forth" to the imagination of the benefactors. Those items, we said, should be
marked with the names of donors, and we promised to

return them when our work was completed.[8] We asked boys and girls, whose generous offers of work could not be accepted because they were too young, to bring the gifts of those who could not bring them themselves. We reminded them not to forget their identity cards. We also asked people to offer food, especially flour and sugar. There were no means of transporting gifts, so every item had to be brought by hand.

My brother Stas was in the neighborhood and just dropped in to see what we were doing. When I told him that our hospital was being born, he volunteered to assume the responsibility of administration. Mrs. Glinski telephoned that men were needed to remove the heavy club furnishings, carpets, and so on, and women were needed to clean the building during the night, before the gifts poured in. Stas said he would go to defense headquarters and get men to do the heavy work. I told Mrs. Glinski I would broadcast our request at six P.M.

I called the radio station and asked the staff to announce the establishment of the hospital and to state that we needed volunteers and equipment; I also told them I would personally broadcast the most urgent needs at six P.M.

There were four French windows back of my desk. While sitting there I became aware that someone was standing behind me, outside the open windows. I turned around to see three schoolgirls. "What do you want, girls?" I asked. "We are not eighteen yet," was the reply. "We want to be useful, but no one will let us help." How very sad, I thought, to feel that one can contribute and be useful, and to be rejected because one is too young. It is everybody's war, and those who feel they can help should be allowed to do so—the very young and the very old. The girls thought that my silence meant another rejection and began to cry. It was as if someone had opened three faucets at the same time. "Please do not send us away," they begged. I realized that we would need three persons to take telephone messages that night, so I took their names. "And now, Sophie, Rose, and Mary, you can go home. Tell your parents where you are working, and at seven o'clock report to Maltanski Hospital. Stand by the telephones, and note every call. I shall see you tonight." They jumped for joy and ran off.

Before Dominik Lempicki returned, all the formalities had been attended to. The hospital was ours, and would be known as "Maltanski Hospital."[9] We briefed each other on the progress of our endeavors. I was very impressed with Dominik's efficiency, courage, sense of responsibility, and foresight.

Josette came back with the typist. An air raid was on, and every now and then a bomb exploded nearby. The typist trembled with fear, but worked on, stuttering on her typewriter—"Heeeeeelp tttttthe woundeeeeeed." She was so nervous that a few sheets were spoiled before a fair copy was obtained. Josette volunteered to take the communiqué to the newspapers. I went to the radio station.

On the air I stated simply that Maltanski Hospital was to be established, that we were asked by the army headquarters to have it functioning by noon the next day, that we needed volunteers for all posts, and that anyone who felt that he or she would fit some particular job should join us. All we could tell them about the work was this: it will not be paid for; it will be very hard; and in it one can be killed or crippled. We wanted everyone to weigh those factors and to realize that the road to the east, out of Warsaw, was still open. "Right now, tonight," I said, "we need women to clean the club after the furniture is removed. We ask them to come with their own pails, brooms, dusters, and soap. Tomorrow morning we will need young and strong hands, boys and girls, to carry gifts to the hospital, as there is no other means of transportation. We need equipment for the hospital. Anyone who feels they have something which we can use, please call us, and we will collect it."

Next, I went to the classroom for the lectures to auxiliary nurses. But there was no lecture that night. Almost all our instructors had been called to their military units. The students were heartbroken when they heard that the courses were closed and would not reopen until further notice. When I told them that we had a new hospital, and that those who wanted to work could begin at once, however, they showed intense relief. So glad were they that there was useful work awaiting them, that most went straight to Maltanski, lest they should miss their chance to enroll.

The hospital was like a beehive. Women came, each with her own equipment. They were from all walks of life—clerks, professional women, socialites, and housemaids. They scrubbed floors, scoured walls, washed windows and staircases, cleansing with a vigor which many possibly never had dreamt they were capable of. All the telephones were busy. Sophie, Rose, and Mary and a few other teenagers took messages.

Some key positions were already filled. Dr. Szymanski took the responsibility for the medical staff. He was a well-known eye surgeon, a professor at the University of Warsaw Medical School, and a Senator. Monsignor Dobiecki, Chaplain of the Order of Malta, came to have a look. He said he would act as hospital chaplain and take responsibility for burying the dead. He realized that we would need a number of stretcher-bearers, and suggested using seminarians. They would be on hand early the next morning, he said, and would help to carry goods until needed for the wounded. Chef Kwiecinski came to have a look at the kitchens and evaluate their potentials. Mr. Kwiecinski was THE chef of Warsaw. He directed the preparation of banquets when then President entertained foreign heads of state. Not only was he resourceful in handling food situations, but his voice, with a quality of thunder, proved invaluable in many situations later during the siege.

Weary, I went home, but just as I was about to fall asleep, the radio accounced that a building in my street was in flames, and called upon neighbors to help. I dressed and hastened to the scene of the fire. At three o'clock in the morning my day was finished at last.

Thursday, September 7, 1939

At about seven in the morning, on my way to the hospital, I was burning with impatience to see what progress had been made on the building during the night. Even from a distance one could tell that many people had visited it during the night, for in front of the doorway lay a great heap of articles, brought, I was later told, by all classes of the community. Inside the hospital I found feverish activity. Even at this early hour several wards were fully prepared, and the others would be soon. I was very happy.

We had to set up some working arrangements and lines of responsibility. The excutive council of the hospital was to consist of my brother Stas, as commandant, and Roman Chlapowski as his assistant; Senator Szymanski as chief physician; Mrs. Barbara Glinski as director of nursing; Monsignor Dobiecki as chaplain; and, without specified posts, Dominik Lempicki, myself, and my assistant Josette Karszo-Siedlewski. We planned to meet twice a day, early in the morning before the first air raid, and in the evening after the last. We agreed that in an emergency any one of us could assume authority in anyone else's domain.

We felt that by noon the hospital could begin to receive the wounded. To have a hospital functioning twenty-two hours after the decision to found it was possible after all.

Before nine o'clock a long line of people had gathered

outside, each with a gift. In the soft air of this beautiful September morning stood rich and poor, old and young, men, women, and children, waiting patiently to hand over their contributions. Here was a small shopkeeper, who brought 2000 zlotys. At the start of the attack, before the banks had closed, he had withdrawn his savings, and now he was offering them to the hospital. He bore himself modestly, as if thankful to us for allowing him to contribute his savings. Behind him came an old woman in shabby, ill-fitting, threadbare clothes, a pensioner. She gave fifty zlotys, her life savings, gathered penny by penny over the years, with the whispered words, "If I had known, I should have saved more." A girl laid her trousseau down before us; it had cost her years of privation.

We gave out receipts at the entrance to the hospital, and then let each person take his gift to the place where it would be used. Each one thus knew where the bed he had brought would stand, on which shelf his pound of sugar would wait its turn to be used, or where his towels would be kept. The manager of a beauty shop not far away gave the nurses' aides white uniforms and also some beauty advice. The aides really seemed to become quite pretty.

Our telephones were busy with offers of gifts and with requests for help in carrying them—the donors wanted to see how their gifts would be used. Calls came from people who offered all they had. A woman, very poor indeed, sent a message to us: she was ill and could not come to the hospital, but she offered her own bed, the only one she had. "Poland's sons," she said, "wounded in defense of their country, shall not want, if someone has what is needed." Such was the spirit that ennobled the mind and strengthened the soul of Warsaw.

The hospital seemed like a great fair, with people coming and going. Some presented us with their gifts, looked around, noticed that something was missing, and hurried back home to return with the needed article. The receipts tell a story of sacrifice, of charity—the work of these Good Samaritans. These gifts were sacrifices that money could not replace, for many stores had been destroyed or closed; there was no transportation; the enemy was already at the gates of the capital; and death from the air had emptied the streets. Not all the goods reached the hospital. Many a donor perished on the way, his mission of mercy known only to God, his offering destroyed by a bomb.

By ten A.M., 300 volunteers for the hospital staff had been accepted and already put to work—doctors, nurses, ward-maids, clerks, kitchen-hands, laundry workers, stretcher-bearers, sentries, messengers, and rescue workers.

I went to Army headquarters to tell the chief of the medical service that by noon we would be ready to take in the wounded, but that we would be unable to carry them to the hospital as we had no gasoline for our few trucks and cars. He told me that they were short of gasoline at headquarters, too. At that moment the telephone rang. The call, from one of the railway stations, requested an ambulance for two wounded soldiers who were bleeding profusely. The reply was that the few ambulances left in Warsaw were engaged in evacuating patients from the Hospital of the Transfiguration, which had been bombed an hour ago. The raid was still in progress; the bridges over the Vistula were being attacked; and it would be impossible for anyone to get through. At this point I intruded. I asked for two drums of gasoline for the use of our hospital, plus the loan of the small Fiat, called "flea" in Poland, that I had noticed in the gateway when I was entering the building. I offered to go for the soldiers myself and take them to our hospital. My proposal was accepted, so I set off immediately with a military driver.

Not a soul was on the streets; Warsaw seemed a city without people. As we were crossing the river a bomb struck the edge of the bridge and exploded in the water. Like a fountain, the water splashed on our Fiat's roof. Just after we had crossed, another bomb landed in the middle of the road, about fifty yards from the end of the bridge. A column of water from a broken water main spurted high into the air and we were splashed again. We passed the zoological garden; a few bombs had landed there and the animals were stampeding in panic; the roar of pain and terror was deafening and heart-rending. Overhead, streetcar cables were twisted menacingly. Bomb craters were numerous.

At last we arrived safely at the station. While the two wounded men were being squeezed into the back of the car, I talked with the stationmaster, who was still in a daze. During the past hour a plane had unloaded its bombs on the station, then had circled and machine-gunned the station from all directions. One of the wounded soldiers we had come to pick up had been hit in the shoulder by a bomb splinter; the other had been shot through the lungs by a machine gun while he was trying to pull his companion to safety. The stationmaster, who had been at this station thirty years and had never held a gun in his hands, had then grabbed the wounded soldier's rifle and shot at the plane, which dived and crashed.

Quite unexpectedly, just as we were about to move off, I was given two stretchers. In the hospital we had stretcher-bearers, but not stretchers, so I was very pleased. The car was too small to carry them, but I could not risk leaving them behind, so I knelt by the car door holding the stretchers outside the windows.

As we bumped over the debris that littered the streets, and dodged the bomb craters, I looked at the two soldiers behind me. They must have been suffering great pain, but their teeth were set, and no murmur came from their lips. I was especially worried about the one shot through the lungs, because he coughed now and again, and each time blood spurted from his wound. To make them feel that there would be an end to our journey, I kept up a running commentary, telling them where we were and how much nearer to the hospital we were coming. As we raced across the bridge a few bombs splashed into the Vistula, but since we were in the open they were not so terrifying. The "all clear" sounded just as we reached the hospital. It was noon.

Those two lads were our first patients. The sounding of the "all clear" at the moment the first transport of wounded stopped at the entrance of the hospital was considered a good omen by the staff. In times like this, when life and death depend on unpredictable coincidences, superstition flourishes.

Since the hospital was open, my assistant, Josette, declared firmly that she would bring in the boy whose wound she had attended the day before. She grabbed the stretcher I had just brought, found two sentries, and went off. They would have to carry the boy about thirty blocks. But the raid was over, and on the way they would find all the helping hands they could use.

My adventures for the day were not yet over. Headquarters called to tell me that the infirmary building of one of the airplane factories still stood, though the factory had been destroyed, and that we could take everything from it that might be of value to the hospital. We set off at once. The grounds and buildings of the factory were deserted. We could hear no human sounds. The walls of the factory stood stark, perforated like sieves, roofless and shattered. Desolation and ruin had reached this busy hive of modern engineering. Death and destruction cast their shadows where but a few days before could be heard the whir of wheels and the hum of voices.

We drew up at a closed iron gate, and I got out and went through a gap in the wall to find myself in a large rectangular court. Red sage in full bloom blazed in the burning sun, riotously defiant in the strange, new wilderness. A crippled truck lay on its side; several empty beer bottles told their own story. I could find no infirmary.

I returned to the airfield, where I was told that the infirmary I was looking for was in the opposite direction. We started off again and soon saw a bomber squadron coming toward us. I prayed that the infirmary would not be hit.

We arrived there unnoticed by the bombers, but the bombing continued. We saw several policemen taking cover in a ditch by the roadside and we jumped in beside them. The bombers were flying so low that we could see the faces of the airmen distinctly. They were encountering no opposition. They were masters of the sky, out for a joy ride. One of the pilots was laughing as he pointed to the destruction beneath him. The bombing went on. I flattened myself in the ditch and offered up prayers for the safety of the infirmary and of our car. Why were they bombing, I wondered? No one and nothing lay below; there was only devastation.

Huge clouds of black smoke could be seen over the city. "That's the third time today," one of the policemen said, "that those devils have been over here."

They might return still again, however, so we hurried to the building and climbed upstairs.

Walking over heaps of broken glass, we reached the infirmary. It looked as if there might have been a surgical operation in progress when the place had been abandoned. Here lay a shoe and a hat, over there a coat. A pool of fresh blood told a tale of horror. I began to take everything I thought might be of use to us, stuffing surgical instruments into the pockets of nurses' coats. We could hear the drone of planes and could see them in the distance, returning toward us. We had to hurry, for around us lay priceless treasures. We worked feverishly. The small car soon was so full that I could not get in, yet I did not wish to leave anything that might prove valuable behind. The policemen lifted me up and pushed me through the window.

The driver was wonderfully cheerful. He told me he was a taxi driver in Zyrardow, a little country seat. He was constantly cool and self-possessed and told me the news as we drove back. "Do you hear the ripping of the machine guns?" he would say. "That is for the benefit of the refugees hiding in the ditches." And again, "Oh, he dives; there will certainly be a bomb, but we shall pass." His judgment was uncanny.

"Dear boy," I implored, "please drive more carefully. I can see nothing, as I am above the windows, and my head strikes the roof with every bump. We may escape the German bombs, but you yourself will knock me out."

At length we reached the hospital safely. Someone opened the door of the car, and to my sorrow a jar of iodine fell on the pavement and broke. It is strange how things register in one's memory. Some happenings, like this incident with the jar of iodine, are still so vivid that I can almost see and feel them, while the picture of the refugees taking shelter in ditches as we drove to the infirmary, their miserable belongings scattered on the road, is blurred in my memory.

When the car had been unloaded at the hospital, we made up our minds to go back again. Mrs. Glinski had made another list of what to look for. On the way I thought we should have something to eat, so I invited the driver to lunch at the Europa Hotel. It was an exclusive place, not one where a taxi driver would usually drop in for a snack. It tickled me a little when the waiters could not conceal their surprise at seeing my companion in his leather coat.

Then it occurred to me that the policemen at the airfield might appreciate some brandy and cakes. The cafe had only twenty cakes left. I asked for them all and was offered five. This, I felt, was not enough for eight men, and after some discussion I walked out with all twenty. When we passed my home, I went in and picked up a bottle of brandy.

We came upon a huge crowd of people watching several policemen lead a spy out of a gate. It was a revolting sight. He did not seem to be a man any longer, but a startled, howling animal, a coward without dignity.

We arrived again at the airplane factory, where the brandy and cakes were most welcomed. What a well equipped infirmary they had there! Shelves reaching to the ceiling were filled with bottles and jars bearing strange inscriptions. Besides a list of medications, I had been told to take anything else that might be useful. "Which among all these bottles with cabalistic signs are most necessary?" I said to myself. The chemical formulas meant nothing to me. Nor did it comfort me in the least to reflect tha if a pharmacist had to choose a concert program in my music library, he would be no less bewildered than I was at this moment. All of us—the eight policemen, the driver, and I—tried to match the inscriptions on the jars and bottles with Mrs. Glinski's list. After loading the medications we still had some room in the car, so we filled the space with iodine, morphine, ether, absorbent cotton, and bandages of all sizes. We placed the bandages and cotton on top of the other supplies so that I would have a soft layer on which to lie down when I was pushed through the window for another drive like the one in the morning. We found some sacks of sugar and flour, and put one of each into the luggage space.

After unloading our supplies at the hospital, we had hoped to return a third time, but it was now too late in the evening, and the barricades were closed. Patrols reported that the Germans were near, probably already at the airplane factory.

The hospital was now functioning, with almost a hundred wounded.

I went to headquarters to report on the day's activities and to thank the staff for the loan of the car. The commandants of all hospitals were required to report each evening on the number of wounded admitted. I had offered to make the report that evening. When the chief of medical service glanced at the report he exclaimed, "What right do you have to admit civilians to a military hospital?" Another officer commented that it was "unheard of." I reminded them that there was no other hospital in the area and that we had decided that any wounded who were brought to us would be attended to. "Do you realize that you might be court-martialed?" someone said. Of course I had not had much military experience—I had been in uniform only a few days. My ways of thinking were not yet structured along those of the military mind. For a moment I was speechless with anger. Then I said, "It is everybody's war, and everybody has an equal right to be helped. In Maltanski, anyhow, that will be done." Getting up, I added, "If you wish to court-martial me, you are at liberty to do so." I left the meeting with a feeling of leaving a stage after the last encore.

I walked home. It was late. I took a warm bath and smoked a good cigarette. I wondered, however, whether they really would court-martial me. I telephoned Stas and Dominik. They both thought I had done the right thing. Stas, as commandant of the hospital, said he would call the hospital and reaffirm this policy so that everyone would be clear that we admit all the wounded. As Malta delegate for Warsaw, Dominik said that he would take this up at the highest level, as it was a thing of principle, and that obsolete army regulations should be changed to accord with circumstances. Reassured, I went to sleep. It was my last night for some time in a real bed. War for me began the next day.

Friday, September 8, 1939

This eighth of September was a lovely day. September is always beautiful in Poland. The air is soft; the sky is pale blue; and the clouds, if any, are small, white, and friendly. The crops are in, and the country people can relax. Everything in September seems to be resting and peaceful. Threads of cobweb move quietly through the air, resting on stubble and bushes.

When I left my apartment to walk to the hospital, I found the streets barricaded. I had to climb over rocks, upset streetcars and automobiles, and piles of rubbish, and I had to jump over trenches.

I wondered what on earth could have happened to the streets.

Later I learned that the night before, some fool had gotten hold of the broadcasting facility, and had asked the people of Warsaw to erect barricades and to dig trenches across the city streets. In their zeal to be helpful, to have an outlet for their anger, and to assuage their fear, the people had done a thorough job—though a senseless one—and transportation had come to a standstill. Our hospital, for example, was practically cut off from the rest of the city.

I needed to stop and think about what to do. I entered the hospital, opened the French doors of what used to be the club's ballroom, and stepped into the garden. Fat pink and bluish drops of dew, suspended on cobwebs, roses, and leaves, glistened; a bird sang, and a dog came to greet me.

Most of our staff were still absent; and we had no idea whether they would be able to reach the hospital. We wondered how we would be able to perform our duties.

The commandant started out towards headquarters to ask for help. In spite of the condition of the streets, in front of the hospital were a number of people bearing gifts. The most precious gifts, six wagons, stood humbly on the square—each with two strong horses and a driver. The drivers were Jews who loaded coal on the outskirts of the city and sold it by the bucket in the slums. They offered the hospital all they had: their horses, their wagons, and themselves.

A telephone call came from headquarters, asking us to pick up a number of wounded solders at one of the railroad stations. No one was there who could administer first aid, and some of the wounded were bleeding badly.

Though none of the staff knew where that railroad station was, Shmool, one of the wagon drivers, did know. Not only did he know where it was, but he also knew all the alleys that no one had bothered to barricade. He was confident that he could get to the station. Josette climbed on the box beside him and they drove away.

We realized then that we would be able to reach the wounded, and we knew that a wagon could carry more people than an ambulance.

Later we learned two more important things. We realized that most of the soldiers, who were country boys, felt more secure in an open wagon than in a closed ambulance. They could see what was happening, and could relax when no immediate danger threatened. The second factor was the drivers' muscles, tremendously strengthened by loading coal. Any one of them could lift a wounded man and place him in the wagon as if he were a baby. This gave added assurance to the wounded that they would be brought safely to the hospital.

Shmool and Josette had a hard time reaching the station. Not only were they faced with the barricaded streets, but with machine-gunning and bombing; for a time they were forced to take shelter in a ditch.

At the railroad station Josette administered first aid as fast as she could; it was important to place the wounded men in the wagon and to move away from the dangerous spot as quickly as possible. Every railroad station was a priority bombing target, even a station of such little strategic importance as this one. The journey back to the hospital was a terrifying ordeal. A plane spotted the wagon and dropped a few bombs; another roared past, raining machine-gun bullets as the wagon jolted along between ammunition dumps. Another pilot dived to almost 300 feet of them, released a bomb . . . and missed. The horses became frantic. The explosion and the debris falling all around were too much for Shmool, too. He unharnessed the horses and rushed them close to a wall for shelter. Josette climbed back over the driver's box and sat among the wounded. She adjusted their bandages, which had been loosened by the rough journey, and comforted them, sustaining their courage and hope. She told them that as long as the driver and the horses were safe they would all have a chance to reach the hospital. This turned the attention of the men to the safety of the horses rather than their own until the raiders had passed. They reached the hospital without further incident.

This had been Josette's first trip under fire. She came through with indomitable resolution and courage, qualities shown in every task she was to undertake. Later, the people of Warsaw called her their "gallant lady." Never did her courage waver.

That morning there was trouble in an important department of the hospital—the kitchen. Among the gifts brought to us that day were sweets. Our oldest staff member, Mrs. Deszert, who had had long experience in charity work, was overjoyed at these very welcome benefactions. She took them to the kitchen, untied the parcels, sorted out the sweets, and made separate heaps for each kind—plain chocolates, nut chocolates, mints, and so on. But the chef had to prepare lunch for several hundred people, and needed space. He pushed all the heaps into a jumbled pile at the end of the table, and was greatly offended that his authority had been undermined. Mrs. Deszert, in turn, felt injured because her work, on which she had expended so much time, patience, and meticulous care, was unceremoniously jumbled up in a twinkling by a majestic sweep of the cook's arms. Some tact

was needed to smooth matters over. But obviously the
kitchen was too small for these two dominant personalities.

Mrs. Deszert retired from the kitchen front to a quieter
department behind the lines, where she repeated her previous performance. When she had finished, she counted the
number of sweets in every mound. Later on, having occasion
to visit the Hospital of the Holy Ghost, in which there were
many injured children, I asked Mrs. Deszert to give me some
sweets to take to them. She sent me a bag, and a card bearing this note: "I enclose forty-seven nut chocolates, twelve
large chocolates, sixty small chocolates, and 135 mint-candies;
total, 254 sweets." Such precision in wartime!

That afternoon, when I was leaving the hospital to report
to headquarters, I noticed a girl struggling to carry a bed
that she was bringing to the hospital. I learned that her name
was Mary Plochocka and that her family was too poor to
give us anything. Mary was disconsolate. She thought that
perhaps some wounded soldier had no bed to rest on. This
so preyed on her mind that she prevailed upon her mother
to allow her to offer her own bed. Mary was determined to
sleep on the floor, so she took her bed and carried it herself
across the city to offer it to the hospital.

As I walked to headquarters, about nine blocks away, I
found the streets deserted, as waves of bombers appeared
over the city. I felt excited, and sometimes ran. A bomb exploded on the pavement in front of me. Two adjoining
shops, a florist's and a hairdresseser's, were demolished. In
the glassless window of the former a large blue flowerpot
with beautiful pink gladioli still stood unbroken; in the latter
—grotesque among shattered glass—a dummy figure stood intact, with red curls and long blue eyelashes, grinning inanely
from among the splintered vanities.

I had been at headquarters only a few minutes when the

telephone rang. I learned that our hospital had just been bombed. Beside myself, I dashed back. I could see planes diving and could not think of what had happened or was happening; the thought burning in my brain was that at that critical moment I was not at my post. At length I reached a spot from where the hospital was visible. I stopped, at first afraid to look. Thank God, the walls still stood and the roof seemed undamaged, though the doors and windows had been blown out. Passing bomb craters, pools of blood, and dead bodies blasted and smashed, I reached the hospital. The bombing was still going on; and rescue teams were bringing in the injured. On the marble flagstones in the hall lay the body of Mary Plochocka, who had brought her bed for a wounded soldier—she would need it no more.

I hastened to the operating theater. In the adjoining hall, in the next room, and on the stairs, lay the dead and the dying. The toll was heavy.

At that tragic moment, a scene struck me as comic. One of the wounded, a young and very fat girl with a slight arm injury but suffering from shock, was careening round and round. The blast had left her with her skirt only an apron in front, but without a vestige of covering behind. Behind her, Monsignor Dobiecki, holding a rug like a toreador, was trying in vain to shield her and protect the innocent eyes of the young seminarians who were working as stretcher-bearers.

I went to direct the rescue work outside the hospital. Casualties were still coming in. The hospital stood at the end of open grounds, making the work of rescue teams particularly hazardous.

When the bombing was over, the planes continued circling, diving from time to time to machine-gun anything that moved.

One of our messenger boys, Boleslaw, ran out with a stretcher to pick up a wounded man, but alone, he was of course unable either to lift the man or to carry him on the stretcher. A passer-by who had sought shelter in a doorway went to help him. Together they moved the wounded man onto the stretcher. Boleslaw took one end and lifted it, but the other end was not raised. The lad turned around to see why and found his helper lying dead on the ground.

By now, as it seemed that everyone who had been wounded in the streets near the hospital had been carried in, I went indoors to see once again whether the operating theater needed help. On the second floor I leaned against the window sill and looked out. Dead bodies were all around, and gifts were scattered.

At the far corner, almost on the square, was something that looked like a coat. What if it was a child? I rushed down the stairs and out to the square. Yes, it was a child, a little Jewish boy. The slums, with a dense Jewish population, were not far away. His wound was gaping and it was obvious he was beyond assistance. He could no longer speak. When he saw me, he lifted his hand and opened it. In his palm was a tiny, one-ounce package of tea he had been carrying to the hospital. It was evidently important to the boy that his mission be completed. I knelt by him, took the package, placed my hand under his head, and said that the gift would reach the hospital as he wished and would be used to comfort a wounded soldier, and that now I would stay with him. The boy relaxed and died in peace.

Years before, strolling in the woods, I had come upon a fight in which a blackbird was killing a young sparrow. When I appeared, the blackbird had released his prey and flew away. The sparrow was shivering with fright when I had picked him up. He had nested in the palm of my hand and died peacefully. I felt that it was a blessing to die in the hand of a friend. Strange how a casual experience suddenly springs back into one's memory with a new significance.

While the life of the boy was ebbing, the planes circled and took turns diving at us. I could hear the changing pitch of a plane preparing to dive, and bullets hitting like dried peas thrown into a saucepan. I could hear the plane approaching along the square toward the boy and me and then go away, again, and again, and again.

Though I knew we were the target, and I was aware of the danger, in a way I was in a world of peace, and felt that the enemy could not reach us. It was a moment of understanding the sanctity and dignity of death. If only once in a lifetime one has offered all that one has, without restrictions, totally and unconditionally, one does not need to sneak out of life by the back door. It does not matter if the sacrifice involves a kingdom or a one-ounce package of tea; it does not matter whether it comes from an older person or from a child. Such a person contributes to the survival on this earth of the highest human values. He will live through the survival of the values he upheld, like the little boy who was killed on a mission of mercy, and whose name I do not know.

I did not want to leave his body in the street until it was dark and safe to remove the bodies of all the persons killed in the afternoon, so I took it in my arms and walked across the square toward the hospital. I could hear the roar of a diving plane and the splatter of bullets. The plane was coming straight at me; I could see the pilot's face. I was in an open space, and he could not possibly miss me. Suddenly his guns stopped; he glided over my head and flew away. People later said that my luck was incredible, that the pilot must have run out of ammunition. But I felt that even in the first impact and excitement of war, this triumphant young Nazi might not have run out of ammunition at all. Perhaps he had only for a minute taken off his mask of warriors, and as a human being silenced his guns out of respect for the sacrifice of a little boy. A little grave, so small, next to that

of Mary Plochocka and near those of countless others, was
dug in our garden, where the red begonias and roses were
blooming so beautifully under the warm sky.

Some might be surprised that we buried our dead in the
garden. But in those few weeks about 100,000 people were
killed in Warsaw. The cemeteries were located on the outskirts of the city, which were in the battle zone. Moreover,
how could we have gotten the dead to the cemeteries? Bodies
were buried in gardens, in any green patch, under pavements
—alone or in common graves. Many were buried under the
debris of crumbled buildings.

Late in the evening the commandant, Josette, four messenger boys, and I sat on the stairs in the darkness. Stuck to
the window sill was a thin candle, its light flickering miserably. We had finished bringing in the dead, and needed some
rest. We began to talk about the raid and the thirty-two
bombs that had been dropped: eight in the square in front
of the hospital, four in the courtyard, and the remainder
scattered. A big bomb remained unexploded, embedded in
the wall of the hospital below the roof. We felt that the
hospital had been spared to carry on its work of mercy.

My hands were dark with blood; my legs were bloodstained; and there was blood inside my shoes. The floor in
the hall was not even, and I had stepped ankle-deep into a
pool of blood.

"Will you have something to eat?" said the commandant,
"I am hungry." We all were very hungry.

On a table in the hall were food parcels that had not yet
been taken to the storeroom. Someone groped among them
and returned with a tall, slim jar of honey, a dry sausage, a
watermelon, and a package of cracknels.

There were no knives, spoons, or napkins. We ate with
our dirty, bloodstained hands, even dipping our fingers into
the honey jar to spread the honey on the cracknels. How

easily one discards sanitation and etiquette when primary needs demand satisfaction! It amazes me to remember how, almost callously, we consumed that meal—with the dead bodies of those who were killed in the hospital lying below us on the marble flagstones.

Someone banged excitedly on the door. Who could it be? It was past ten. A woman entered, and approached us with rapid steps, almost running, to offer thirty-six zlotys ($5.50), collected among her neighbors. That woman lived in a very poor quarter, miles away. She had come in the darkness to do her bit for the wounded. She poured out some words of excuse for coming so late in a single breath. With that, she was gone, before we could say "thank you."

Monsignor Dobiecki took charge of the dead. The hall had to be put in order before the morning raid, which we knew would come without fail. The dead had to be searched for identification. Dominik joined us, and we helped Monsignor in his task. It was a harrowing experience, searching the pockets of the mangled dead, through clothing saturated with blood. Each body was examined, and all that was found was tied up and carefully labeled—photographs of dear ones, rings, bills, wallets, and even the receipts we had given in return for generous gifts. The bodies were then taken to an empty house next to the hospital. They would be buried when the sun rose, before the first enemy raid. After we finshed this work, we cleaned the hall thoroughly.

The air raid was over. But then something demolished a wall of the house next door, leaving a dense cloud of dust. What could it be? Half a minute later we heard a whistling sound, followed by an explosion. For the first time artillery fire had begun, coming from the west. A few days later it came from the north; afterwards from all sides, without interruption—day and night, day and night.

I suggested to Josette that she come with me to visit the operating theater, which was then on the second floor. We went upstairs, Josette a few steps behind me. Scarcely had we reached the landing of the second floor, when a bomb which we had overlooked, resting just outside the French windows of the hall, exploded with a terrifying crash. We were lifted into the air and shot over the banisters, landing on the marble flagstones on the other side of the hall. "My God!" I heard the commandant shriek, "They are killed." I first thought that I really had been killed; then I realized that I was alive but lying on someone. The voice of Josette then came from beneath me, "No, I am not killed, only wounded in the back." "I shall try to relieve you of my weight," I said, "but I am hurt in the back also." With some difficulty we got up, moved about a few times, and realized that we were not injured at all.

The German artillery later that night was more nerve-racking than the crash of bombs. We were not yet accustomed to the sudden burstings and the continuous roar.

Someone was banging on the front door, which was locked to protect us from saboteurs. "I am Roman Chlapowski," the voice said. We knew him; I had danced with him at the United States Embassy not long before. "My first-aid post on the outskirts," he told us when he came in, "has been blown to pieces. If you need me I shall remain here with you. If not, I shall rest and find some other duty tomorrow." He then stretched himself on the billiard table and immediately fell asleep. The commandant looked at Roman, sleeping, and said that it was impudent of him to occupy the billiard table where he himself had hoped to sleep. I had had the same idea. Sitting in a large chair in the hall had to substitute for the luxury of stretching out on the billiard table.

What a restless night it was! I made a few rounds through the wards. At the end of its second day of existence the hospital was already crowded. As the artillery fire intensified, my fear increased. Until then, war had been an adventure, and an exciting one, even the events of that day. That night it dawned upon me that the adventure was over; it was no more a matter of my playing a spectacular role, but rather a reality in which I had assumed responsibility. That night I stepped out of my youth.

Saturday, September 9, 1939

Dawn broke with the rumble of wheels and the heavy tread of men. I went out and found a group of policemen with a carload of bedlinen for us. "Sixteenth precinct police station sends these gifts to the hospital," announced the leader. They unloaded the cargo on the lawn and were off. This was such a precious gift that it had to be brought in under cover at once, for the raiders might appear at any moment, and a white spot like the bedlinen would attract their attention. (We thought that the Red Cross sign, which had been placed flat on the roof yesterday before noon, might have been responsible for the bombing we had undergone. We removed it, as it seemed that each day a new hospital was selected for destruction.)

I was reluctant to wake up anyone to help me for this short time, as dawn was an interim when the staff could have some rest. At this point two young people appeared from nowhere. They told me they were brother and sister, students at Poznan University, and had walked all the way from their native town. The boy was eighteen; he was hoping to join the army later. The girl was twenty. They wanted us to accept their help. I said that there was work to be done right away, and pointed at the heap on the lawn. Together we carried the linen into the hospital. This done, I took the girl and boy to have something warm to eat after their long trek, and to have the staff find jobs for them. They both remained with us.

It must have been six A.M. when Dominik rushed in, saying, "Come along quickly; here is something wonderful!" We hurried out, and on the square saw to our joy two magnificent young chestnut horses, without harnesses. Surely Providence had sent them to us! Transporting the wounded and bringing supplies to the hospital had presented continuously increasing difficulties. Getting hold of the horses, however, was a tricky problem. They had been frightened by the bursting shells, and galloped away whenever we drew near them.

Not far away there was a smashed ammunition cart, in which I hoped to find something that could be used as a bridle. A shell burst nearby; a man passing sank to the ground. Carrying some straps, I rushed to his aid, but when I reached him he was dead.

I returned to the scene of action. A shell struck a pine tree some distance from the ground, and the upper portion fell with a crash that put the horses into a frenzy. We began to despair of ever catching them. "Perhaps water will do the trick," Dominik suggested. A messenger brought me a pail of water. I stood coaxingly before the animals, showing them the pail, and then poured a litttle water onto the ground. The horses became curious and less excited. Then I walked slowly backward, still coaxing them toward me. They fell into the trap beautifully, and were soon in a passage-way between the hospital and a neighboring house. Dominik and the messengers devised a door for this improvised stable from some broken beds, picked out of the debris. The horses soon quieted down, feeling themselves safely at home.

Every day things like this happened—strange, unaccountable things that no one could fathom. Where did those horses come from? Whom or what did they draw? From where did the ammunition cart come? It was as if walking through the forest on a fine morning, one came across a tangled heap of torn and blood-spotted feathers. We would know that a tragedy in the bird world had taken place, but would know nothing of the details.

Not far away was a smashed, green one-horse cart, with a Red Cross emblem painted over the name of a breadshop. I went to have a look; maybe we could use it. Inside was a big, thick rubber glove and a straw mattress. We took the latter, rejoicing that the horses would have a one-course breakfast.

I remained behind and sat on one of the cart's shafts to have a rest from people and from responsibility. Something was not right; there was a need for adjustment, for regaining a sense of proportion. I felt an oppressive feeling of guilt, and it made me angry. Why should I feel that way? What had I done to make myself feel like this? Maybe it was childish to play treasure-hunt for the horses. What was wrong with it? This was the time of day when we could rest; the shelling was sparse, only an explosion here and there. Our night work was over.

When I left the office everyone was relaxing. Senator Szymanski was playing solitaire. Stas was shaving himself with cold water and discussing elaborate dishes with Mrs. Glinski, who was smoking a cigarette, her feet up on my desk. Josette was adjusting her make-up and lamenting that she had delayed getting a permanent wave. Now, she was asking, when could she possibly get one? Roman was polishing his shoes.

What was wrong? In front of me was the square, quiet and deserted. The rubble from collapsed and half-burned houes, the abandoned ammunition cart, and the body of the man who had been killed less than an hour before blended before my eyes.

What is it in a human being that finally will bring to mind a failure, in spite of all efforts at avoidance and rationalization? I began to see the dead man much more clearly than the things around him. As far as any spectator could have told, I had rushed to help the man. Still, I sensed that my feeling of guilt was connected to him. Could I have helped him in any way? No, half of his head had already been gone. If there had been a spark of life in him I would have brought him into the hospital. Then where did I fail? I felt that I had failed in humanity, if only for a moment. When I ran to help the man I had thought, "Why does he have to be wounded here just now?" I had felt relief that I did not have to bother with him, as the dead outside the hospital were not our responsibility. I could go ahead with my little fun with the chestnut horses. It was not gratifying to recall those strange thoughts. When our executive council met, I told my colleagues about the incident, as I felt it might be helpful to them.

Toward noon, while I was away from the hospital, ammunition wagons stopped near our door. Their horses, I was told later, were exhausted, so the commandant gave the ammunition men our two horses. I was glad that I had been away at the time.

Till now we had not arranged any place for the staff to rest, sleep, or dine. In any case there was very little time for rest; work kept rolling in. We ate where we could and slept where we were. But this could not continue. We had planned to use as staff quarters a house next door, but it collapsed, so we had to start planning again.

When we had originally set up the hospital, a place had been designated as the staff dining room. We had expected to seat the staff in two or three shifts. That room, a corner room, with French windows and a balcony, had been chosen because it had an esthetic view. We thought it would be an ideal place to relax. Perhaps it would have been if the artillery fire had not interfered. Before noon shrapnel came through the window, and a few shells struck. We abandoned the whole idea of having a dining room, as we realized that before long we might not even have food. So far we had had only a small ration of bread and a bowl of whatever Chef Kwiecinski could supply.

We placed a few benches in the spacious coal cellar to serve as our dining hall. The staff preferred to gaze at coal in safety rather than to be hit with shrapnel while admiring an esthetic view. Chief Kwiecinski designated one of his helpers to keep a candle burning in the dining cellar around the clock.

The safest places in the hospital were the wine cellars, deep underground, large, and windowless. It was true the air was stale and damp, but at least explosions could not be heard. We decided to place children and the oldest members of our staff there.

Our oldest staff member, Mrs. Deszert, was seventy-two years old. To be accepted as a member of our volunteer war service only one qualification had to be met—usefulness and willingness to work. Mrs. Deszert had spent the previous night sleeping in a rocking chair in a ward, the part of the building most exposed to enemy artillery. When she learned that she was to sleep in safety in a wine cellar, she became indignant. She had chosen to sleep in the ward because she felt it would raise the morale of the wounded. They would think that because she was there, it must be the safest place in the hospital. The cellar, Mrs. Deszert said, is for the children—she is a soldier. She insisted she needed no bed, that a nap would be quite sufficient for her. She had found a perfect place for herself, she said, the chair in the ward. "Are we in a hospital or the Ritz? Did I come to help the wounded or not?" Either she would stay there, or . . . Mrs. Deszert would not let anyone argue with her, not even the chaplain.

It is one thing to be a healthy soldier, upheld by a cause and by the fight itself. It is quite another thing to be a wounded soldier, helpless and defenceless. A wounded soldier suffers; he hears planes droning overhead; he knows the pilots are searching for a target. Hospitals are targets; perhaps that pilot is trying to locate our hospital, he thinks. He hears the bursting of shells and bombs, the crash of falling houses. Now he can hear better because the windows have been blown out. Each day he opens his eyes to find fresh holes in the walls caused by shrapnel; frequently pieces of shrapnel are swept up from the floor of his ward. Candles are not needed at night because the wards are lit up by the blaze of burning buildings.

The only hope of safety for a wounded soldier is with the nurse. Not only will she take care of his wounds, she will not desert him—she will save him.

Maltanski Hospital was blessed because our volunteers were true as steel. During the bombing of the afternoon before some members of our staff had lost their nerves, and had left the hospital. As soon one person left, however, another would step into her place. After that, we knew that those who remained after their baptism of fire and fear could be relied upon.

In spite of great weariness, the nurses always appeared cheerful and tranquil. No thoughts of shelter for them, even if they trembled with fright, even if their hearts were filled with terrible anxiety for their families. They had to hide their fears. With confidence and strength of character they had to encourage those under their care. The ward is a citadel in which the nurse has responsibility, even if she is just a very young girl.

That day it seemed that the personality of the city changed. During the previous few days one could hardly move through the streets. Now all those who sought safety in Eastern Poland had left the city. The stream of refugees from the west had ceased. There seemed to be two categories of people in the city, the defenders and those who had buried themselves as deeply as they could in cellars or whatever other shelters they could find. A spirit of determination and sacrifice inspired the defenders of Warsaw.

Josette came to my office, so angry that she almost cried. The issue was gasoline. According to my agreement with headquarters, made two days before, I was to receive two drums of gasoline if I managed to take care of the two wounded soldiers at the railroad station. I had delegated to Josette the job of getting the gasoline. When, however, she went to headquarters, she was given a requisition coupon instead of gasoline. The sentries were assigned to accompany her out of the city to an army dump, where she was to carry away as much gasoline as could be loaded onto a wagon. Half of it, though, was to go to headquarters.

The day before, Josette had gone on her errand, a mission far more hazardous than my dash across the bombed bridge to the station. Her group had been attacked by planes and, carrying a substantial load of gasoline, had had to evade German patrols. The expedition had taken the whole afternoon. When they had returned to the hospital, the bombing was over. We had planned to take our part of the gasoline before the next day's morning air raid and give headquarters their share. That evening, however, when artillery fire started, we had dared not risk an explosion in our yard of thousands of gallons of gasoline. Therefore, we had sent the whole load to headquarters for storage.

The following day, when Josette went to take the part that belonged to us, she found that all the gasoline had been disposed of. She was given another set of requisition coupons and once again started for the army dump. But the dump had been blown up. What upset Josette more than anything else was that she had to return empty-handed. She would not give up, so with Roman, she again walked to headquarters. Her determination finally was rewarded. They were given what gasoline was available—four one-gallon cans, which they carried back to the hospial. For the sake of four gallons of gasoline, twelve lives had been risked: two lives on the first trip, four on the second, four on the third, and two on the fourth. Life seemed to be growing cheaper every day. I realized, however, that the bargain would enable me to go to the railroad station and save two more wounded. Moreover, it provided me with a most exciting adventure that I would never have wished to miss, so I bore no grudge. What about Josette's part? She laughed and said it was fun, parts of it, especially dodging the German patrols.

As I went through the wards I noticed a young nurse looking very pale. "What is the matter, nurse? Are you very tired?" "My father has been killed," she replied. "Wounded soldiers from his regiment who were brought here told me how he fell and gave me his watch." She continued working; no one else in the ward knew how she was suffering. In the evening I called her to my office, which was then in a telephone booth, and gave a glass of wine. During this short break, she gave vent to her sorrow before returning for night duty.

In the afternoon a rumor spread that England's Royal Air Force had bombed Berlin. All of Warsaw was electrified; people talked of nothing else. We did not mind the bombing that afternoon, as we felt that the Germans would now get more than they gave. Now they would learn something!

I was out most of that day, occupied with rescue parties and organization work. I spent the night in the hospital, and made it a point to visit each ward three times. There was no rush, and I had time to talk with nurses and give them a hand when necessary. Each time I visited a ward, another patient had died. The nurse and I would carry the bodies out—the stretcher-bearers were so exhausted after the day's work that it would have been cruel to wake them just when they had the opportunity to snatch a little rest. Sometimes it was a soldier who had died—he had done his duty and he knew why he died. But most terrible of all was to carry the body of a child—how heavy those small bodies were! There was something so shameful in it.

That night a little girl called to me from her bed. She had a smashed leg, and her side was terribly injured. I sat on her bed, took her in my arms, and asked whether the pain was very bad. "No," she replied, "but I should so much like to see my mother." I knew that I would not be able to fulfill her wish; her mother and little brother were lying in our yard, killed in the afternoon raid. But I noted her address and planned to try to find some member of her family the next morning. When I was about to leave, the girl asked whether I would return. I nodded my head. "Then I will wait for you," she said. My heart contracted with anguish, because I had heard those exact words that very afternoon.

I had been returning with a car loaded with seriously wounded men, when a little girl had waved to me to stop. Her mother, she said, was very ill. I had gone inside her house and found that the woman was in labor. I had told her that as soon as we reached the hospital I would send some-one to help her. The child had asked me whether I would return, I said I would. "Then I will wait for you," she had said.

I had fished out of my pocket a little bracelet of red beads and slipped it on her wrist, saying it would help me to see her from a distance and find the house easily.

I could not stay long, for the wounded were bleeding severely. Transportation was so difficult that we could only take patients who were hemorrhaging in cars. Others had to be carried in horse-drawn wagons. In normal times each of the four wounded men piled in the back of my car would have been on stretchers and rushed smoothly to the hospital in an ambulance with all the necessary attention. But these were abnormal times. Many a wounded person who had been pushed into the back of a car died when when the car bumped over debris or a hole. Most fainted; that at least saved them the pain of later being pulled out of the car.

While the wounded were being unloaded from the car, I had found a doctor to go with me to the woman in labor. I had not noted the exact location of the house, leaving the responsibility to the driver. When he stopped the car and seemed puzzled, I thought at first he had lost his way. There was no house, only a heap of debris. Certainly this could not be the right place. Then I had seen, on a battered lilac bush, the torn-off hand of a child, with a bracelet of red beads.

Several times that night I returned to the ward where the other little girl who had said she would wait for me was lying, to reassure myself that she was still alive.

Before dawn things quieted. I sat down with the nurse in charge of the ward. She said that I had made her burden lighter by my concern for the wounded little girl, and she wondered why she felt that way. So many of us, I thought, do not realize that whatever we do, we should do it in the name of God first of all. One is so often ashamed of some belief, lest others think it ridiculous, that he refrains from admitting what he really feels. As I looked at the nurse I felt that she had taken off the mask that she had molded to make her appear aloof and authoritative. We talked not as two masks, but as one human being to another. I said that my compassion and concern alone would not be strong enough for all who needed it. I was certain that at that moment I drew on the compassion of all those in the world who keep vigil and pray and have compassion, so that I could use it at any time for those who needed it.

Sunday, September 10, 1939

In the morning, and again in the afternoon, a number of churches were bombed. We wondered whether it was accidental.

I was told at headquarters about an enemy bomber, shot down on the outskirts of the city, whose pilot was killed. Inside the plane our soldiers founds a wounded woman. She apparently had gone for a jolly raid. Only a few moments before this plane had bombed a church and had machine-gunned women and children who were running for cover. One of our soldiers who took the woman out of the plane asked her how she could bomb women and children. "Have you a heart?" he continued. "I am only sorry," she replied, "that we were not able to drop all our bombs, and use all our bullets." Forestalling any idea of taking her into Mal-tanski, I commented that it would not be pleasant for any-one in charge of a ward to have this patient, and departed.

We still had newspapers, which now were delivered free at about noon. They were really more like bulletins or leaf-lets, because they had only one page, with no advertisements, of course. The editors realized the tremendous importance of familiar newspapers for the morale of a city. Distribu-tion, of course, presented a special problem. I do not know how the whole process was handled; all I know is that hands were stretched out to grab this small bit of evidence of civilization, and that it meant much to us.

That day's newspaper said:

> On the 8th September, the enemy bombed the center of town and buildings of historical importance. The bombing of these densely populated areas cannot be justified, as they are far from the Vistula bridges and are of no importance in defense.
>
> Yesterday 100 tanks were attacking on the outskirts of Warsaw; twenty of them were destroyed by our aircraft and artillery fire. Seventeen airplanes were shot down by our aircraft. Two airmen, Suchecki and Koreywo, each accounted for six.
>
> The Germans fight well, and do not surrender.
>
> One officer, taken prisoner, admitted that the war was not popular in Germany.
>
> Chancellor Hitler spoke in the Sports Palace yesterday. He denied that open towns had been bombed, and said they would not be. In an appeal to the British and French armies he declared that he did not wish to annex any British or French territory.
>
> President Starzynski calls upon the citizens of Warsaw to work and resist. He tells us in his speech that we shall win, and that Warsaw must be defended. If civilians and persons in uniform will stand together in the service of Poland, victory will be assured.

In the afternoon we received a call saying that reinforcements were needed to help one of our rescue teams evacuate wounded from a church. I was free, and so I gathered the available men, and went to lend a hand. The area was being shelled; and the shells whistled by. I had not known that my brother Stas was in charge of the operation, so I was surprised to see him. Stas was a typical Foreign Office man, never in a hurry, with excellent manners. He could master any language in a few weeks. I had tought he was sissy. But I could see him now, standing in the open, directing the action as nonchalantly as if he were a host at a party. I reported our arrival to him, but I could not listen to him, for the whistling of the shells made me nervous. I asked whether we might move close to the wall. He said no, it would be inappropriate; a leader must be seen and heard by his men. We will talk here, he said, adding that when one hears the whistling, the shell is already past. If I would only stiffen the muscles of my neck, he said, my head would be held upright. I stayed with him in the open for practice.

Toward midnight, after I had made the rounds of the wards, my hopes for a rest were dashed by an order from headquarters to transport wounded from a field hospital at Warsaw's outskirts to the auxiliary hospital in the University of Warsaw. After that I was to report to headquarters.

I searched for my driver of several days, Zwerdling, and at last found him, sleeping in a hall. He was a very pious Jew. Never a morning passed without Zwerdling, in ritual dress, carrying out the Talmudic prescriptions.

When we went into especially dangerous areas, I would pray aloud. Sometimes, when it seemed to Zwerdling that it was very dangerous and I was not praying, he would call out: "It is time to invoke Mr. God; it is time to invoke Mr. God!" I said a litany, and Zwerdling answered, "Have mercy on us, Commandant."

Driving that night was very difficult; it was very dark, and heavy patches of smoke drifted down onto the streets. One square became enshrouded in a particularly thick cloud, just as some soldiers were marching through. As we drove along, a fifth columnist threw a hand grenade onto the road. It burst some yards ahead of us without doing any damage.

Frequently shots were heard in the dark. Three times in

the previous few days I had been shot at from behind. It was unwise to travel at night without a gun. An officer who was brought to our hospital had been wounded in the arm by a fifth columnist. The thing to do, we learned, was to turn around and fire in the direction from which the shot came. Then one could proceed unmolested, because when a fifth columnist knew his target was armed, he would not dare come into the open.

We drove through fire and smoke, guided by dim streaks of shining light on the streetcar tracks, but we met much heavy debris and many bomb craters.

Breathing at times became painful. The air was saturated with smoke and with the smell of burning human flesh.

We stopped at one point because of mines, and tried the next street, but had to stop again for the same reason. We drove back to find another way and squeezed between barricades. At last we reached a long avenue where, ahead of us, fighting was going on. Having the road free, we speeded away from the dense smoke. The road was being shelled, and machine-gun fire could be heard.

Machine-gun fire did not distress me; it was insolent and gay. As for bombing, one saw the plane, heard the bomb, knew when danger was near, and knew when it had passed. Artillery fire, however, made me despair; one never knew what direction it came from. I was terribly frightened of it, and always shall be.

At the field hospital carts, trucks, and ambulances had already been loaded with mangled human flesh by the time we arrived. Six men, seriously wounded, were pushed into our car; there was no ambulance to take them, and we could not leave them to die on the road. Our army was falling back; the enemy's artillery fire drew nearer. The road by which we had come was now impassable. We were trapped.

Time was racing against us. We would all be killed if we did not move. Our only chance was to cross an open field.

The sentry declared that no one in his senses would travel that way; it was mined, and there was only a footpath, which could not be seen in the darkness.

I had once seen wounds caused by mines, for a number of our soldiers had entered minefields by mistake. They were all killed, their bodies terribly lacerated with strange wounds —small metal circles, embedded deeply in the flesh, with pieces of metal pointing in different directions, like a ring with keys attached.

As there was no other way to go back to the city, I decided to go through that field, and gave the command, "In the name of God, let us start!"

Zwerdling, who had been listening to the sentry's remarks, was visibly afraid. I feared that at any moment he might abandon the car in panic and take to his heels. Without a driver we would all be killed, and our car would be left as a menace to other traffic. Shells were bursting around us. I got out of the car and lit a cigarette. "Listen, Zwerdling," I said. "I shall walk before the car; you will see the glow of my cigarette. If I pass through, you can safely follow. If anything happens to me, you drive on to the University of Warsaw."

I walked forward, covered by dust thrown up by exploding shells. Moving mechanically, with my mind a blank, unable to pray, unable to think, I was not even frightened. I was just an automaton. I did not know whether I was on a footpath or not. There were blasts and crashes in the pitch-black night. It is impossible fully to express it in words, but of this I was convinced: I was led, and I followed blindly, to safety.

When we reached the other side of the field, I took my place again in the car and fell fast asleep. I was awakened by a jolt as we stopped in the university courtyard.

The Sisters of Charity had taken charge of this auxiliary hospital. Those who were off duty slept on the corridor floor. One, with an eye to comfort, had chosen a corner by the fireplace. Presently a shell struck the chimney, and sent the soot flying all over her. When she awakened and joined the others —they had been called to receive a fresh batch of the wounded —she did not know what an amazing apparition she appeared. We had great fun, but for the poor sister it was a catastrophe, for she knew the difficulty of getting water—not to mention clean clothes.

I reported to headquarters the safe arrival of all the wounded. It was about three A.M. I found the major in charge doubled up on a small sofa, his head resting awkwardly on the sofa's wooden arm, with the light from a strong lamp shining straight into his eyes. As I entered he awoke like a man roused from a drunken slumber. He tried to pull himself together and follow what I was saying, but obviously was too worn out. Knowing that he had not left the office for ten days, I felt great compassion for him. Finding a pillow in the next room, I put it on the arm of the sofa, and he immediately fell asleep. I wrote out the report, leaving it on his desk, put out the light, and returned to the hosptial. Strange burning marks were on my forehead and under my left eye, but I was much too tired to bother, and soon fell asleep.

Monday, September 11, 1939

Fifth columnists caused us a great loss. Our new three-ton truck, sheltered in a nearby gateway, was found with its engine filled with sand, and all its wires cut.

Today's press clippings:

> In obstinate fighting at Warsaw, the Germans suffered heavy losses.

Warsaw yesterday had a bad day, being bombed 14 times. Fifteen planes were shot down.

At Marymont [on the outskirts of the city] a tank attack was repulsed. Some Germans taken prisoner did not know that France and Britain had declared war on Germany.

Paris, 9-11. In France, a Polish army is being formed under Polish command.

The British Empire is at war with Germany.

We work for peace—on the barricades, and on the field of action. Warsaw roaring with explosions, strewn with pieces of shells, choked with smoke. The face of the capital is beyond recognition.

The Hospital of the Transfiguration, in Praga, and the Marshal Pilsudzki Hospital were bombed.

People standing in queues for bread were machine-gunned.

People in the streets were machine-gunned, too.

The Germany Embassy has been destroyed by artillery fire.

Seventy enemy divisions are in Poland.

The Germany claim that Warsaw has surrendered. This is not true; our men fight on.

President Stephan Starzynski,[10] the mayor of Warsaw, gave us courage and hope in his speeches. The mayor of Warsaw was called "President"; this title, however, was always coupled with his name, to avoid confusion with the President of Poland, who also resided in Warsaw.

President Starzynski was an excellent administrator, and he adored the capital with the devotion of a young lover.

Warsaw was a city one could love. It was the heart of the nation, not its arsenal. This was clear when one walked in Saski Garden, founded in 1729—the first public park in Europe—where nightingales sang, hidden in lilac bushes that were so old they had grown into trees; or when one drove through the city and noticed the absence of statues of generals on horseback. In Warsaw one would come across memorials of Nikolaus Copernicus holding a globe, Frederic Chopin, Adam Mickiewicz, and Marie Curie-Sklodowska. We honored thinkers and artists, those who contributed to our betterment as human beings. Except in 1938, when we infamously snatched a piece of Czechoslovakia, Poland never waged an aggressive war. We were not warriors, but we had to fight to protect our cultural heritage even if it cost our lives.

President Starzynski spoke to the people of Warsaw several times a day. "We have given flour to the bakeries," he said that morning. "There will be bread for all. You can have meat too. Make soup for a day. Save for the army defending the capital. Do not drink liquor. The Germans drink liquor. They need stimulants; we do not. Everyone should stay at his post."

And, in the afternoon: "This is not the end of the world; neither is it the end of history. The bombing of the civilian population and of open towns dishonors the German nation. It will cost Germany dearly. I have received a letter from one of our officers telling me: 'The battalion is transferring its pay to the children of Warsaw.' The soldiers fighting think of the children of the capital. With such men we shall win. Work battalions are now organized. All the firemen from other towns are ordered to join the Warsaw fire brigade."

President Starzynski's personal enemies were the raiders, which bombed the public utilities at least three times every day. Telephone lines were severed; electric power was cut off; and water mains were burst. But owing to the mayor's gigantic efforts, as soon as the bombers flew away squadrons of repairmen went to work to keep the utilities functioning.

A message came from headquarters: "Go to the customhouse; it is on fire. Take what food you can for the hospital." I went out to look for the cars, but found only the small

Fiat. Leaving instructions to hold all cars that came in till my return, I set off, taking two messengers.

On arrival at the customhouse we found several wooden buildings on fire. Fortunately for our purposes the fires were in places where agricultural machines and other things we were not interested in were stored. We took three bicycles, on which the boys set off for Maltanski, leaving room in the car for as much olive oil as we could carry. Back at the hospital, we found the truck and the large Buick, and left in the three cars, with Dominik and four men carrying hatchets.

Though the fires had made little progress, a plane circled low overhead, waiting to machine-gun anyone who recklessly ventured out.

I had imagined a customhouse to be a place at the border, where a polite man tried to prevent your escaping payment of extra duties on your treasures. I had not realized that a customhouse actually includes endless storehouses, railroad cars, and so forth. On entering and looking round, I felt like Gulliver among the giants.

Dominik and I separated, each of us taking two men, and we arranged to meet in an hour. My party entered a storehouse, and found innumerable crates. When we broke some open as we went along, however, we discovered to our despair that they contained French silk! No use to us! We hopefully opened another set of crates, but found only optical instruments. And so we continued to spurn measureless wealth, which shortly would be reduced to ashes. Our luck turned at last; we found coffee, bags and bags of it.

A little further on we came across hundreds of barrels of wine, one with the top off. I took a cup for myself, then handed one to each of the men. I could feel the air shot through with electricity; it was a chance in a lifetime to those poor, hungry, anxious men, who knew not if they would be alive in an hour, to have a barrel of excellent Chablis at their disposal and within easy reach. It was a crucial moment in my expedition, and I feared for the men. "Now lads," I said, "There's a quart of brandy for you tonight, so make haste. Take a few barrels of wine to the truck, and let us get off!" Avoiding further temptation, I struck the barrel with a hatchet, and the wine gushed to the ground.

As the men carried the coffee to the truck, I searched still further. I pried one crate open with a hatchet, put my hand in carefully, and drew out a handful of raisins. A Red Cross man appeared, and asked, "Can you let me have half of the raisins?" "Yes," I answered quickly, "but tell me, where is the cocoa?" We counted the crates of raisins and took twelve crates to the truck. Then we went in search of the cocoa, which was in another storehouse. We ran, keeping close to the wall to escape the bullets.

The plane circled very low, then flew upwards. We hoped the pilot would fly away, but he came at us again, only from a different direction. Sometimes he would glide noiselessly along just above the housetops, and then unexpectedly spring out and shower bullets on us. Or, he would climb and then go into a deep dive with the engines roaring at a high pitch, and then turn on his side and without a shot slide away in a semi-circle just for the fun of it, like a cat playing with a mouse. I wondered whether he realized that we were human beings. Then came a surprise for both us and the German pilot. One of our military patrol trucks, armed with a machine gun, arrived. The plane, unaware of the truck's presence, was diving; our gunner fired, and with his first shots stopped the game. The plane crashed, bursting into flames outside the customhouse gates. We were happy, very much so—glad that the villain had been punished, and that we would be safe from him. We did not think of him as a human being dying in a burning plane. Now we could move safely.

We found the cocoa, and met Dominik returning from another part of the establishment with tea and other treasures.

There was still some room in the cars, so we looked for prunes, which the chef had especially asked us to get because the hospital stores had none. "Dominik, did you see prunes anywhere?" I asked. "No," he replied, "but let us go and hunt for them, as our last search before we return."

I went toward the railroad siding. A wasp brushed past me. I wondered if it would guide me. I pursued it until I found myself walking knee-deep in peanuts, which had fallen from a smashed railroad car. I had lost the wasp, but I knew my goal could not be far away. Another wasp! And then more, all flying in the same direction—and so we found the prunes.

Without further adventure we reached Maltanski.

An hour later the supplies had been stored and an inventory list handed in at the office. Looking through the list, I noticed: "Raisins, eight crates." What had happened? I might have miscounted other item, but I was sure we had brought twelve crates of raisins. "What exactly do you mean by eight crates of raisins?" I asked the storekeeper. "I brought twelve." "Indeep, you brought twelve crates," he replied, "but only eight were of raisins. The other four contained telephone dials." Oh!

All through the day my vision had been blurring, and the brown patches under my left eye and on my forehead, which I had noticed the night before on my return from duty, were burning.

Late in the afternoon I went to headquarters for a conference. I could hardly see, and wondered whether the reason was lack of sleep. Coming out of the conference I suddenly saw flames and then only darkness. I heard a familiar voice greeting me by name, and recognized Colonel Rostworowski. "I cannot see you, Colonel," I said. "Would you be so kind as to call the military policeman to lead me out? Something queer has happened to my eyes, and I cannot see." A hand guided me. It was a strange sensation to walk without seeing. Distances are very deceptive; the car was waiting just round the corner, but it seemed a tremendous way off.

I heard Zwerdling jump out of the car. "What . . ." but his question remained incompleted, as my guide evidently signalled him.

Zwerdling at the wheel usually twittered like a sparrow, but now he was silent. Stas was waiting at the entrance of the hospital, for they had telephoned him from headquarters. He took my arm and led me to the operating theater. I sensed that several people were around, although no one spoke.

That afternoon it was reported to headquarters that a number of people had suffered severe burns. Apparently the night before the Germans had used artillery shells filled with mustard gas. As I had been walking through the mine fields, guiding the vehicles that carried the wounded, a few droplets of the gas had apparently hit my face. The characteristically delayed reaction was affecting my eyes.

Later I rested in our infirmary. An antidote for mustard gas had been applied to my eyes, which were covered with poultices. My head felt very tired.

One does not need sight to sense another's concern, and I could feel that Dr. Szymanski, a professor of ophthalmology, who was treating my eyes, was not hopeful. He relied on his experience, but I relied on my feelings. I felt sure that it was a temporary condition. I thought that perhaps I had been unable to tolerate what I had been seeing, and so, had subconsciously drawn this curtain before my eyes. The fact that I was in darkness did not disturb me just then, because at this time of the evening it was dark anyhow, and I had learned to move around efficiently in blackness.

Having rested comfortably for some time, I thought it would be advisable, while alone, to try to find out if I still could be useful, in case I did not regain my sight. Against the wall I knew there should be a cabinet containing surgical

instruments. I felt my way and came upon it without difficulty. Then I opened its door and passed my hand over the
instruments. Thank God! I could name them all. I was happy.
"Now," I asked myself, "would it be possible to feel my way,
open the door, and reach my office, across the corridor?" I
went to the door, turned the handle without groping for it,
and walked straight to my desk. Someone entered, and,
though not a word was spoken, I knew who it was.

At nine o'clock that night the regular executive council
meeting was held. As each person entered, I could tell who he
was, and where he seated himself. My sensitivity grew con-
siderably. A new sense came to my assistance—something that
is impossible to explain.

That night I did not go around the wards; Josette replaced me.

Those rounds were important for the morale of the nursing staff. They felt that we cared, and would come immediately to their assistance if necessary. These young girls carried
a tremendous responsibility. Often they had to make instantaneous decisions, which would be made in normal times
after deliberation by a team of specialists. To listen without
impatience or haste to their difficulties, fears, achievements,
and hopes and to give them recognition for their efforts, their
endurance, and their courage, helped them. Experienced
nurses suffered from feelings of guilt. They were trained to
know what a medical decision is, and taught that a nurse never
makes medical decisions. They felt very guilty when the circumstances compelled them to break their tradition.

We constantly impressed upon everyone who worked in
the Malta Corps that failure lies only in neglect, when one did
not do what all that was humanly possible under the circumstances. That, of course, was easier understood intellec-
tually than accepted emotionally. That is why nightly rounds
were most helpful—to lighten the burden through understanding and the magic of recognition.

There was a lull in the artillery bombardment in our area, so I could relax. Still in the office, I turned on the radio. An excellent pianist was playing Chopin's Concerto in E Minor. The music was coming to me from far away; it was soothing, like a ray of sunlight in a dungeon. How far, I thought, can we reach with our modern means to communicate at a distance, to express ourselves in a way that can build up or destroy! What a great responsibility it places on the individual whose message can be heard by anyone!

Music provides such an excellent background for daydreaming that my mind wandered back to an earlier time, when I was a pianist, days that now seemed far away, as if in someone else's life. I recalled that my last appearance had been with the Warsaw Philharmonic Orchestra; I played Bach's Concerto in D Minor. When I received the press clippings and placed them in my file, they had taken up the last space. I had wondered if it were an omen.

The Chopin concerto to which I was listening came to an end. It must have been relayed from a concert hall, because the applause could be heard. I felt left out, not being able to join in the ovation; how out of place it would have been for me to clap where I was! I thanked him mentally, therefore, from the bottom of my heart, and felt certain that this concert was for me, although the pianist, of course, did not know it. I understood at that time the power of a "thank you," and that in reality my "thank you" was a prayer. Thanking the artist, I could not disregard those who had taught him and those who had organized the performance, and the conductor and every member of the orchestra, and their teachers and the ones who had constructed the piano and all the other instruments, or had built the concert hall. What about the discoverers of waves that could be harnessed so that tones could be sent into the air and picked up in some distant place? How about those who had built the radio station or who had supplied the necessary materials?

What about the shopkeeper who recently had loaded a wagon with radio sets and come into this office, saying that he wondered whether radios could be used in hospitals? He installed most of them in the wards, but saved one for the office. "I know it is not the usual thing to have in an office," he said, "but everything is so unusual, and it might be useful, perhaps." When I began to think of all who had contributed to make it possible for me to listen to this concert, I realized that a person who is thanked is like the captain of a team that receives a trophy.

One day recently a young boy was brought to our hospital with his chest so badly injured that he was beyond assistance. His face was contorted with pain. A nurse came to relieve him with morphine. He tried to say something, and she bent down to catch the words. "I am dying," he whispered, "I won't be able to do anything more for Poland—do not give me—the injection — because — I — offered — my sufferings — to God — for — Poland."

I thought of Maltanski Hospital and of its work, realizing that though it had been functioning for only five days, I had seen more humanity, more devotion to duty and sacrifice there than in my whole previous life. I had never thought it was possible for human beings to have such qualities, and to such an extent. I thought of what was going on in the hospital that night, and of people who came to give their own selves and how different they were from those who were merely trying to save their lives in shelters.

Since the first bombs fell on Warsaw I had been in constant movement. For what purpose was I stopped now, and would it be a temporary affliction, or would I have to readjust my whole way of living? What would life demand from me under these circumstances? Mrs. Glinski came to change my dressings, as the burns were painful. I then had the luxury of a few hours of uninterrupted sleep.

Tuesday, September 12, 1939

Throughout the morning I worked in the office on a variety of problems Corporal Uptas had brought me. The messenger boys—twelve to fourteen years old—and the sentries, of whom he was in charge, looked up to him because he was courageous, and had confidence in him because he cared about them.

Corporal Uptas told me about three of the boys, John, Andrew, and Mike.

For the past three days John had suffered cuts that looked as though they had come from rolling in broken glass. He came from a very poor family, and wanted to gallivant on bicycles like the other messenger boys, but had never had an opportunity to ride one. He had decided to learn how. Seeking privacy, he chose to practice, of all places, on the glass roof of the bank at the corner of the square. Luckily he had escaped only with cuts, and had not fallen four stories.

The corporal next told me about Andrew, who was twelve years old and was feeling bad because he was small and often taken for only ten. When he was sent on a mission, he would plan carefully, and ask what he should do in case the situation should change. He was so reliable! Corporal Uptas said that Andrew would take a little bite of his bread ration and hide the rest, and that at night he sobbed. The corporal thought that they boy worried about his family, and that he took his food ration to them.

Before I talked with the boys, the corporal and I decided that it was advisable to ask the secretaries to send John on a mission that required a long bicycle ride, so that he could establish status with the messengers' group and not feel it necessary to prove himself by riding on a glass roof. If we had made an issue of his riding on the glass roof, and disciplined him, we would have achieved nothing. He would have defeated us in some other way. He had shown that his imagination in choosing ways to establish status was ingenious. We had to respect the need a boy had at that age felt to belong and not to be considered a sissy.

We felt that now that I was available, I should see not only the three boys Uptas had mentioned, but all of the messengers, and talk with them individually. That was a function that my loss of sight would not hinder. As a musician with absolute pitch, I was always able to perceive nuances in the vibrations around a person. This quality enabled me to be aware of people and things without depending on my sight. Now, undoubtedly, that ability had increased.

After Uptas left, I talked with each of the messengers in turn.

John came first. He said in a matter-of-fact voice, with an undertone of happiness and pride, that he would have to leave shortly to take a message to the Praga district, across the Vistula. Though Miss Maciejewska, the secretary, had urged him to be sure and get there before the noon raid, he said he was not afraid of bombing. I said that it was not a matter of being afraid or not, that I was afraid myself when I was out where bombs rained. It was a matter of completing the mission.

Then John talked about his family. His parents were dead and he lived with a sister, who supported the two of them by prostitution. Not that John saw anything odd in that occupation; his concern was that he was only fourteen and he would have to wait two more years before he would be allowed to work.

He said that he had come to the hospital because he had heard that in Maltanski princesses and counts worked like ordinary people, and he thought it might be easy to pilfer something. When he came to us, he saw that people were allowed to go through the wards, and that rather than taking things, they looked to see if there was anything needed that they could spare.

He started to show people around as other boys did, and came to feel he belonged there. No one beat him or pushed him around, and he felt as if he were a count himself. We talked about stealing and how easy it was, how things that did not belong to us often just pushed themselves into our hands. But in Maltanski we could not steal; we came not to take but to give. I pointed out his contribution as a messenger, which surprised him greatly. We finished our talk with a pledge that no matter how easy it was, we would not steal. I asked him why he had told me about his stealing, as no one knew of it. It was because it happened so long ago, John replied. Then he had been someone else. It made me smile because this "long ago" was only six days before.

When I talked with Andrew, I inquired about his family. I learned that his mother, a widow, and his sister, eight years old, had taken shelter in a coal cellar, near the hospital, and they had only the food that he could share with them. He worried greatly about them. I asked him whether his mother could come and see me. He went out and soon brought her to my office. I asked her whether she would like to make use of our shelter, which was also a cellar but more spacious. She declined my offer, saying that it had taken so many sacrifices to acquire her furniture that she wanted to keep a close eye on it. It did worry her, however, that Andrew had to deprive himself of his food, little as it was. I told her that Andrew was such a valuable member of our corps that we would share our food with her as long as it lasted. Later Corporal Uptas said that the following night Andrew had not sobbed.[11]

Though the third boy, Mike, did not seem to have any unusual and urgent problems, he worried me. He was under great stress and made light of everything, giggling inappropriately. I did not know how to handle him. But on account of my training in music, my ears detected enough dissonances to make me feel that we should keep an eye on him, and perhaps, when sending him into the city, should be more selective in his assignments.

Except for Mike, each boy had taken off his mask of warriors and had become himself. I could feel the moment it happened and wondered what made it so easy, whether it was that an authority with blind eyes was not threatening, or that he realized that I was as vulnerable as anyone else. It was true that I too had discarded my mask of warriors. I was not pretending to be anyone but a human being who wished to be helpful. I felt very humble because I well realized that I did not know much about the mores and ways of thinking of the urchins of Warsaw, and I was concerned about whether I could convince the boys that I really wished to help them.

At the executive conference that morning it became clear that our hospital was overcrowded and that we needed to establish another one.

In the afternoon I went to bring bread from an auxiliary hospital located in a high school. Arrangements for distribution of food were changing constantly. That day, hospitals had to collect bread from that auxiliary hospital, and someone representing each hospital had to be present to accept it.

I had never noticed this school before, although it was next to the art gallery. What I noticed now, climbing three flights of stairs, was that the steps were very high, and I wondered whether that was usual in schools. I signed the necessary forms and was waiting in the hall for the cargo to be loaded, when I heard a familiar voice greeting me. It was a surprise to meet Grzegorz Fitelberg, the famous conductor. "What are you doing here, Fit?" I asked. "What happened to you? Why are your eyes bandaged?" he asked in reply. He told me that his wife was seriously wounded . . . she was dying. It had happened when they were crossing the bridge over the Vistula. They had a very lovely home in a residential section overlooking the river, and had been told it would be dangerous to remain in that area, for it would be an obvious enemy target. They took their cherished dog, and some overnight things in a valise, and left for the city. (As it happened, their home survived the siege intact, except for a few windows that were broken.) His wife's main worry in her half-conscious state was the fate of their dog, and she constantly asked whether he had been found.

Fitelberg had volunteered his services as a stretcher-bearer. Stretcher-bearing demanded more physical effort than any other hospital job, since elevators often were unavailable or, as in auxiliary hospitals, there were no arrangements for taking stretchers into the elevator. The work never ended. The stretcher-bearers had to carry the wounded out of the ambulances or cars to a designated floor, then to the operating theater, and later back again. They also had to pick the wounded up in the street. Such was the task that Fitelberg, a man over fifty, Poland's greatest conductor, had undertaken. Besides appreciation for a great artist, I felt personally indebted towards him, because he had conducted my first appearance as a pianist and had carried me through Cesar Franck's Symphonic Variations. That concert had opened the doors to what successes I had attained.

Before leaving the school, I learned that two large containers of ether had been set aside there for our hospital. We needed ether badly, but all the space was taken by bread. The previous experience with the gasoline, however, had taught me a lesson—never to leave anything behind, whatever the sacrifice.

Since I could not see, I could not lead the convoy that day. It was the duty of the leader of the convoy to decide what route to follow, when to move on and when to take shelter; to jump out of the car and remove trees lying across the road; and to push unexploded bombs or artillery missiles out of the way. Since I could not do those things that day, I let my place in the front seat be taken by containers of ether, and walked to Maltanski.

It was warm in the sun, but I was greatly afraid. There was

so much debris lying about, and there were so many craters. The shells, hissing through the air, made me nervous.

I set out, feeling the edge of the pavement with a walking stick. Then I became unsure of the streets. Again and again a charitable hand guided me across the road, or took me part of the way; sometimes it was the firm, strong hand of a soldier or a policeman, sometimes a woman's hand, and sometimes a child's. How grateful I was to those good, careful hands!

A number of stores had supplied us with radio sets, which were installed in the wards. It was a great relief for the wounded to have music all day; it helped to drown out the humming of planes and the whistling of artillery shells.

Three times a day silence reigned in the wards, the groans of the wounded were restrained, and the staff crossed the wards on tiptoe while we listened to President Starzynski, the mayor of Warsaw, his tired voice weary to the point of hoarseness. President Starzynski, this gentle, unassuming, and humble man, was the greatest hero of the siege of Warsaw.

His wishes and suggestions were carried out immediately. No one was more trusted. He was worshipped. He became for us a symbol of what Warsaw and we stood for.

President Starzynski asked that the streets of the city be swept during the night, that the bodies of the dead and the carcasses of horses be taken away, and the bomb craters in the roads be filled up. At dark, after the last bomber flew away, people took brooms and spades and worked in front of their own homes and those of neighbors who were absent, or in front of the houses that had become rubble. Every morning Warsaw became more devastated; still, every morning the streets were swept clean.

In the evening there was nothing for me to do. Josette took over and I decided that as the apartment house in which I lived

was still standing, although windowless, I would go home and
pass this one night in real comfort. A hospital car was going
somewhere and took me home on the way. The driver went
with me to my apartment, the door of which had been blown
open by a blast. I asked him to describe the state of the inte-
rior. A shell had entered through the window of my studio,
pierced the wall, gone into the kitchen, and exploded there.
Another shell was imbedded in the same wall. My two pianos
were telescoped into one. When my escort left I found the
keyboard and played a chord; the notes that came out were
false and distorted; the resonance board must have been
broken. It was disappointing, as I felt that to play a little
would restore the harmony in me. Several times during the
day I had wanted to take off the bandages to find out whether
I could see. Now that it was dark outside, my personal darkness disturbed me no longer.

No one seemed to be in any of the top-floor apartments, and
the feeling of solitude was dreadful. Between the houses the
shells were bursting; echoes multiplied the noise, making it
intolerable. In my uniform I lay down on my bed and tried
to sleep, but I stayed wide awake and frightened—more and
more frightened. In the hospital, I thought, we were not so
afraid; we had a purpose in being and living, and felt safe.

It was said in Warsaw that Maltanski was safe from destruction because it had come from the golden hearts of our people.

My fear became more than I could bear; I could not stay
alone any longer. I tried to call the hospital, but the telephone
was dead. I would have to walk. The distance was about
twenty blocks, but as soon as I began to plan, I felt much better. Perhaps I could reach headquarters, I thought; it was on
the way and they would call Maltanski. This morning's experience had taught me that as long as I kept on streets it was safe,
but at crossings and open spaces I was easily confused. To
headquarters the distance was nine blocks, with only one
square, but Copernicus's monument stood in that square. If I

got lost I would bump into the statue and figure out the right direction from how it was standing.

Without too great difficulty and with Nicolaus Copernicus' guidance I reached headquarters. Dominik soon was coming to take me to the hospital. He could not use gasoline, for there was such a shortage, so he had to walk. While waiting for him I talked with headquarters staff—those who usually met there for conferences.

How true it was, I thought, that verbal problems have to have verbal solutions, action problems action solutions, and structural problems structural solutions. On the surface my relationship with the headquarters staff remained unchanged, but I felt that their having cheated us of the gasoline and my insulting them all in the matter of admitting civilians into a military hospital had left an undercurrent of mutual bitterness. There was no better moment to improve relations than the present one. I told them that I felt bad about having handled the matter the way I had. The culprit who had taken our gasoline said he felt bad too, but that he had thought that Josette would be able to get to the depot once again, and that it had been headquarters' intention to let us have all that she would get. Everyone felt relieved, and the cloud of hurt lifted.

When Dominik came, we started on our way. I thanked him for having walked the nine blocks. Dominik stopped and said, "Do you know that a week ago I would not have walked half a block for you even in the most beautiful sunshine?" I said that his feelings toward me before the war had been reciprocated; that it was only a week since we had walked out of the office to look for a suitable building, and that from then on my respect for him had been growing.

Later on that night someone entered the office. A voice said, "It is I, John, the messenger boy." I could detect a note of mystery and excitement. "I recognize you, John," I said. "Why are you not asleep? It is so late." "I wanted to find you alone. Did you ever in your life see a real pineapple? Because, you see, I was sent this afternoon to the Hotel Bristol, and the waiter gave me a slice of pineapple. He said that as it would only be burned, it would be better for me to enjoy it. Have you ever tasted pineapple? It is for you; you have surely never had anything so good. I tasted a small bit, but so small that you could not find the place." And John pushed into my hand a piece of pineapple wrapped in newspaper, still warm from having been carried for hours in his pocket, and quickly ran away.

Mrs. Glinski came to change my dressings. It seemed that the day of surprises was not over. I was actually to have a "room" to myself; a corner under a staircase, about seven feet long and five feet wide, without any window. It was a place where brooms and dusters had been stored. A bed was put there, or rather half a bed, because it was part of a camp bed, about three feet long. But with an added chair it made a more comfortable couch than the office chair, on which I had been passing the nights until now.

Wednesday, September 13, 1939

This day the first week of our hospital's work ended—a week that had seemed like years.

In the past two days many people had come to offer us their services. The news about the loss of my sight had spread through Warsaw and doubled the flow of applications. Many people, realizing that we needed replacements, left the safety of shelters to join our corps. We decided to go ahead with two hospitals, one for civilians only. After each raid we had received many wounded civilians, but had had nowhere to place them. Headquarters, knowing that Maltanski's population had more than doubled, no longer directed convoys of wounded to us. But anyone who was wounded within a reasonable range was brought to us and was accepted.

I went with the commandant in the morning to city hall to confer with President Starzynski about the hospital for civilians. We planned to have ward space and an accident room; patients requiring surgery still would be brought to Maltanski. Details were discussed with President Starzynski's assistant, Mr. Okolokulak, and he was to call on us early in the afternoon. Scarcely had we returned to Maltanski when a message came from President Starzynski, telling us that Mr. Okolokulak had been killed at his desk by shrapnel that came in through his window, and that we should go ahead with whatever plans we had.

Mrs. Glinski was concerned about a situation in ward number six. A few hours after Maltanski became a hospital two wounded soldiers had been brought to us, accompanied by armed guards. Both had been court-martialed and were to be executed within hours. A bomb had hit the prison and they were wounded, and therefore, were brought to the nearest military hospital, which happened to be ours. Armed guards stood by their beds. The commandant persuaded headquarters to have the guards removed, because both men were seriously wounded and there was no possibility of their leaving. The presence of armed guards was also unnecessary and disturbed everyone in the ward. The commandant asked that either the prisoners or the guards be removed, and said that he was willing to accept responsibility for the situation. His vague promise satisfied the military regulations, and the guards were removed.

One of the court-martialed men had shot his superior officer. He insisted that it was by mistake. We believed this, and were glad when after the siege he walked out of our hospital free.[12]

The other prisoner seemed to be a human monster. His face and its expression were frightening and repulsive. As soon as he had joined his army unit and received a rifle, he had robbed a village store, first killing the owners—man and wife—and several children. In his primitive thinking he figured that as long as he was in the hospital he was safe. But the nursing staff represented for him the dreaded authority who would kill him as soon as he recovered. He hated them and fought them by all the means he could, and a bedridden patient can do that by the most primitive means.

When the noon bombing was over, we invited all the ward number six staff for a cup of coffee and a glass of wine. We had almost no food, but our supplies of coffee, tea, and wine were adequate. Everyone from the executive council who could spare half an hour was present. We gave the ward number six staff recognition for carrying out their duties under such unforeseen circumstances. We wanted them to know that we understood how distressing it was to risk their lives for someone they knew was a degenerate criminal. We appreciated that they did not discriminate against him, but simply treated him like a human being in need.

Headquarters called me to ask us to take over an auxiliary hospital. They felt that if we could take the leadership and put a few of our staff in key positions, that the new hospital could function efficiently. It was vital, they said, to have every willing hand used efficiently and every bed occupied. Maltanski's executive council, I felt, should decide this matter, and I asked that an emergency meeting be held when the afternoon bombing had ended. Before we had time to consider the matter, headquarters notified us that the auxiliary hospital had been demolished in the afternoon raid.

A press clipping from Kurjer Poranny (the Morning Courier):

Such are the women of Warsaw:

In the streets crowds of people are moving—mostly refugees from the west. Determination and confidence can be read in their eyes, but their faces are very tired, and their swollen feet hardly leave the pavement. It is necessary to give these people rest and a little hot food, and surround them with an atmosphere of good will and brotherhood.

The women of Warsaw of their own free will undertake this national duty. Today in every street they organize centers for soldiers and refugees, where rest and comfort can be obtained.

At every street corner are improvised stalls, on which the passers-by place what they can—sugar, bread, dressings, clothing, sweets. When a soldier comes from the front lines, hands are held out with warm welcome, and cigarettes are offered.

The housewives try to slip parcels to the soldiers on guard, depriving themselves and their families even of necessities.

In answer to a radio appeal by the Red Cross, announcing that the new auxiliary hospital in the University of Warsaw buildings needed linen and dressings, crowds of women willingly brought everything suitable they could find in their homes.

The women of Warsaw are not afraid of bombs and explosions; they do not grudge their last bit of food, which they share with the defenders of the capital.

Such are the women of Warsaw in the moment of trial and danger.

Though I had moved to Warsaw only a year before the attack, the experiences of the past twelve days had sealed my relationship with the city. From then on I considered myself a woman of Warsaw. That press item about the women, which took one-third of the space in that day's edition of the Morning Courier, impressed me greatly and moved me almost to

tears when it was read to me. Later on, however, it occurred
to me that the "new" auxiliary hospital in the university had
been functioning before the item was written, for I had
brought a convoy of wonded there several days before. Also
there were no more crowds of people moving in the streets;
the streets were deserted most of the time. The western part
of the country was occupied by the enemy and there were no
refugees. I realized that it was a story true in content, but not
in time. However, the women who read it undoubtedly felt
better because they had been recognized. Therefore, I kept
my observations on the inaccuracies to myself.

In the afternoon the dressings on my eyes were changed. I
could see with the right eye, but light was painful to me, and
I needed dark spectacles. I could see with the left eye, too,
but its vision was still blurred and the burn was inflamed;
therefore the dressing was to be kept on for a day or two
longer. This did not matter any more; than God I could enter
once more the active ranks of our team!

Many of the wounded soldiers who were brought to Maltanski and other hospitals reported that the Germans took
women and children from the villages and tied them in front
of their tanks, so that if our soldiers shot at them, they would
kill their own women and children first.

When I first heard about that on the seventh of the month
from the policemen at the airplane factory, I thought it incredible. But soldiers from different regiments and different
parts of Poland reported the same story. Such things had been
known in our history since the year 1109, when the Germans
advanced to the town of Glogow (Silesia) and took the children of the citizenry as hostages. The King of Poland, Boleslaw, ordered the town to hold out. The Germans accordingly
placed the hostages before their front lines, so that if the

citizens dared to shoot, their own children would be killed first.

For two and a half hours in the afternoon, the bombing was very heavy. Over 200 planes were over the city this time; there were many casualties. The wounded brought to us seemed numberless. Along the halls, passages, and staircases, every corner was filled. In the hall forty-two wounded were placed on the floor; eight of them died almost immediately. Operations were performed on two tables at the same time in the operating theater. Help had to be given at once, for the victims were losing so much blood that their lives were ebbing away.

The consensus of the medical staff was that amputations would be performed only when the limb, though attached to the body, was actually dead, or when there was no hope of saving the limb by any means. Young doctors and senior medical students stretched the idea of "any" means very far. They built the oddest looking contraptions, using bricks and pieces of broken beds and pipes. Some wards came to look like junk shops.

A boy member of our rescue team, seriously wounded, had been taken to a nearby hospital. His father came to us in distress, begging for help. His son, a college student, was to have both arms amputated. A horse-drawn wagon was available, and a young and daring doctor went to bring the boy to us. For the next few weeks the boy went through a great test of endurance. The device designed for him seemed like a pillory. He was tied onto it standing; when he was tired and wanted to rest, a few bricks were placed under the legs of a chair so that he could be seated.[13]

In the night I went around the wards. I first removed the dressings from my eyes, because I felt it would be better for the morale of the wounded; in the dim light of a candle my burns did not show. I did not think it would harm me to be without dressings for an hour or so.

My purpose in going through the wards was to help the nursing staff. Yet everyone was so glad to see me, both the staff and the wounded, that I wondered who was helping whom. In one ward the nurses' staff told me how much better they had felt after our coffee and talk in the afternoon.

"Lombroso," as the wounded murderer was referred to by the medical staff, followed me with his eyes, with a look of hatred and suspicion.

Thursday, September 14, 1939

Early in the morning a wagon with two horses brought more wounded people. I happened to be at the door when the commandant came out to receive the wounded. While they were being taken out of the cart, a burst of shrapnel killed the horses. "Young, fat horses," said the commandant significantly, looking at me; we understood each other. I went to the kitchen to see chef Kwiecinski. "Chef," I said, "Shrapnel has just killed two 'cows'; do you think you could send for the butcher to take the meat and have it salted?" Two weeks before, such a proposition made to Chef Kwiecinski might have brought on an attack of apoplexy from pure indignation, but now he considered it a good idea. What a relief for us to have so much more food.

We were hungry, terribly hungry; we had very little bread, only one small piece a day for each of us. One could cut it into thre parts and make three meals of it. Each of us, however, would eat the whole bread ration as soon as we received it. Twice a day we were given also a cup of cocoa made with hot water, sometimes with some sugar.

That day we had excellent soup at noon. Chef Kwiecinski had proved to be THE CHEF once again. There was so much of it that everyone could have a second helping. We called it "neighing soup"; it was made from the remains of our brother horses, sacrificed on the field of honor. It was so pleasant not to be hungry for a while. One could feel that the pulse of the hospital had strengthened.

During the night we went to look for more dead horses. We found three, tied them to the backs of the cars, and dragged them to Maltanski while their meat was still fresh. We were not the only ones who had this brilliant idea; we came across some horses whose flesh had already been removed. Soon we might not have this source of food.

At midday, while we were working in the vicinity of the Saski Garden—such a place of beauty—the hideous Summer Theater was hit. When we saw it burning we were pleased. That scarecrow of a building had been always a blot on Warsaw. It was called "summer" theater, but had a winter season also. Articles had been published in the newspapers over the years, as long as I could remember, vigorously condemning it, saying that it disgraced Warsaw, that it was unsafe, that in case of fire . . . and so on. Nevertheless, the theater had stood, and, as the acting was superb, we willingly went there. That day it had received a direct hit, and a pillar of fire and smoke rose from it. One of my fellow-workers saluted the plane, thanking it for its service. We became a little sad, however, for the theater burned for twenty-two minutes, and filled the whole Saski Garden with smoke and soot.

Stray dogs were running about the city. Some of them were beautiful creatures, others simply mongrels; all were mad with fright and hunger.

A greyhound rushed into the hospital. He questioned every

one with his eyes. It was pathetic. Did he seek someone? Was he trying to escape from something? He rushed out again, seeking his destination.

Chef Kwiecinski had a beautiful pointer whose reaction to raids was puzzling. About a quarter of an hour before the sirens wailed their warning, he went into a frenzy from fear, trying to hide under various objects. When the siege was coming to an end his nose was bleeding—he had been trying to push himself under the concrete floor of the kitchen. We felt that his sensitivity was at a higher level than ours and that he could hear the planes before we did. Shortly before the end of a bombing, which usually lasted between one and three hours—none of us would know how long it would last "this time"—the dog would leave his shelter and unmistakingly manifest joy. How did he know?

Several severely wounded soldiers, brought from a wrecked field hospital, were lying on stretchers in the hall. During the brief formalities of writing down their names and taking their firearms and uniforms for storage, a nurse said to one of the wounded, "Here is your uniform all right, but where are your boots?" The poor boy seemed momentarily embarrassed, and then replied: "I have no legs."

Mrs. Glinski's son had been killed during a night attack. A searchlight had shone on the young captain, and he was machine-gunned. He was not brought to us, but buried somewhere in a common grave, which his mother would never find.

Mrs. Glinski's face became a little more lined, but nobody in the hospital knew of her pain.

That night Josette told me that she must sleep; she had been on duty two days and two nights. She brought a mattress to my "room"—the broom closet under the staircase—put it on the floor, and undressed herself for the first time that week.

Later, when I came in to rest for an hour, she was sound asleep.

Unfortunately I had a nightmare, and began to call, "Josette! Josette! Evacuate the wounded quickly! Put out the cigarettes! There will be an explosion!" Josette jumped up, dressed herself in a minute, and then saw that I was asleep. She was terribly cross, and shook me till I woke up. "Evacuate whom? What will be blown up?" At last I understood, and apologized. "I am sorry, Josette. It was a dream."

We had to keep the door to the hall opened for air, and the wind whistled through the hall's broken windows. Josette and I began to talk about what we should eat when the siege was over. We were hungry, and we imagined twelve-course meals, with such splendid dishes that we were seized by fits of laughter.

Our relaxation and recreation lay in talking about food. Everyone talked about it.

After midnight a courier from headquarters rushed into the hospital, and exclaimed, "In twenty minutes trucks will be sent to evacuate the hospital!" Then he vanished. We held a short conference. It might be sabotage, it might be a misunderstanding; or, it might be that headquarters had learned that we were to be bombed. Since the telephone exchange was not working that night, the commandant immediately went to headquarters to find out the meaning of this message. I called the roll of the whole staff, and minutes after the alarm message everyone was at his post.

The commandant returned. The message was not that the hospital had to be evacuated, but that trucks would come to take the less seriously wounded and the convalescent out of the city.

There was apparently a corridor in the enemy encirclement of the city, leading to a town about fifty miles east of Warsaw, where the evacuated patients could be cared for.

This operation started in the morning. Roman, as assistant to the commandant, led the convoy of those to be evacuated to the specified meeting point, some barracks, but when the convoy arrived they found the place burned down and were obliged to return. We contacted headquarters and were notified that another effort would be made to carry out the plan; the meeting place this time would be the historic Citadel. The enemy must have been notified about this plan to bring certain patients from all the hospitals to one place—soldiers who in the near future might return to combat. Roman's convoy could not reach the Citadel, for the building had suffered a very heavy raid. He returned with his group once again, with only slight casualties suffered in the futile expedition.

As the attempt to assemble the patients at a meeting point had failed, headquarters issued orders to take them out of the city from the various hospitals in smaller groups. We, civilians in uniform, appreciated the value of such a move, because experience had taught us that large groupings of soldiers were obvious bombing targets.

The trucks arrived that evening and we loaded the patients into them. The glare of the city fires was so bright that one could have read small print. The trucks moved on as we called out, "Good luck, boys, God bless you!"

We learned later that this convoy had slipped out of the city without casualties and reached its destination.

We stayed outside a short while. Some drops of rain fell, and how welcome they were. We hoped that at last we should have the much needed rain. In September it usually rains at night, but this year, when we needed rain so badly, there was not a drop.

We did not mind fires any longer, except those that were direct and immediate threats to life. But smoke was unavoidable, for the air was saturated with it. Breathing was painful.

If rain would come we could breathe fresh air, without smoke, if only for a short while. Our hopes were short-lived. Just those few big drops came, and then the rain stopped.

The staff was certain that our alert was merely a rehearsal for carrying our emergency evacuation plan. But in fact, we would not think of depriving them of rest for a rehearsal. Since our alert was interpreted that way, however, we let it be, and praised the staff for their efficient response.

The staff had an understanding that in case any one of us became wounded he would let the hospital know, so he could be brought back to the hospital. If we did not receive a message we were to understand that the person was dead. As for the messengers, however, we took more responsibility, tracing their routes in advance. If a messenger did not return on time we went to search for him.

That evening we learned that Andrew, who had been sent on an errand in the afternoon, was missing. In planning such errands we usually made allowance for the time an air raid lasted, and instructed the boys to take shelter. After all possible delays had been taken into account someone went to find out if the boy had gone to his home. His mother had not seen him. We asked the broadcasting station for help, and every half hour his description was given and his possible whereabouts stated, but without result.

When the evacuation of selected patients was completed, we went over the route Andrew was to have followed and calculated where he should have been when the raid started. A rescue party set out with instructions to search all houses that had collapsed during the afternoon raid in the area. We later congratulated ourselves for having taken those precautions for the messengers, because it did not take long for the rescue team to find Andrew, trapped in the cellar of a house that had collapsed. We sent reinforcements with necessary equipment. Soon Andrew and all those with him crawled out through a passage that our rescue team had opened.

Friday, September 15, 1939

A report of the rescue of little Andrew was broadcast the next morning, and it may have alleviated the anxiety of numerous mothers whose sons worked as special messengers.

When those boys went on errands, their originality in dealing when the unexpected happened was admirable. They combined childlike vivacity with the mature judgment of an adult. But in spite of our instructions concerning sticking to the route, taking shelter, and so on, we never knew whether they would return. When we needed a message delivered, it was difficult to choose which boy to send, for all were keen to go. If they saw one of us coming into the hall where their "depot" was, they would push forward in the hope of being the lucky chosen one.

Their most important work was to act in place of destroyed telephones. Every day we could lift the receiver and find silence, indicating that the telephone exchange had been hit during the last bombing, or by artillery fire. Whether it would be repaired we did not know. Also, many people were staying in their cellars, where there were, of course, no telephones. The only reliable means of communication was a message delivered by hand.

A few days before, one of our messenger boys, Stephek, was sent to buy nails. A heavy raid was in progress. Finding that the shop selling nails had been destroyed, on his own initiative he went to the outskirts to buy them. Coming back, he tied a paper bag full of nails to the back of his bicycle. Unfortunately, owing to the rough road, the nails broke through the paper without the boy knowing it. When he reached the hospital and saw that there was only a handful of nails left, Stephek became desperate. As he was a street urchin, this waste of valuable goods seemed to him to be the loss of a fortune to the hospital. In his eagerness to make up for the loss, before anyone realized what he intended to do, he foolhardily dashed out towards the outskirts again, in spite of the bombardment.

That morning the staff had extra work nailing planks up to block the windows. Since the previous week, when all the glass in the windows had been broken, the wind had blown through the hospital; several of the wounded became stricken with pneumonia.

I found on my desk a typed note which read, "I have a terrible craving for a piece of candy, angel. Can you get me one?" Instead of a signature was Monsignor Dobiecki's seal as chaplain of the Sovereign Order of the Knights of Malta. When Monsignor came to the office I told him that I would do my best to get him a piece of candy, as it had been some time since I was referred to as an angel. Monsignor tore the note from my hand and rushed out like a hurricane. Before evening there was a statement on my desk in official language: "My investigations disclose that your brother, my confrere, the commandant of Maltanski Hospital, tried to improve his skill in typing while waiting for members of the executive council to gather, and typed this note to your assisttant, Josette Karszo-Siedlewski. I thought it was a piece of scrap paper and used it to dry the seal. I hope this explanation will satisfy you." I was entirely satisfied, although I had not complained in the first place.

The commandant came to the office, trying to act naturally, but there was mystery in the air; all present were burning with anticipation. He solemnly walked to his desk, turned over a few notes, and then whispered, "I have bought a cow." We jumped up. "When?" "Where is she?" He replied, "In front of the hospital." We rushed out but found no trace of the cow. There was consternation, and we told him his joke was in poor taste. "But it was there," the commandant insisted. "I paid 400 zlotys for it! It could not disappear into the sky."

Who had seen the cow? Someone said he saw a peasant taking it into a neighboring theater. Incredible! But a real milk-giving cow was in itself an incredible phenomenon, so without any further questions we all rushed to the theater. A torn placard bore an advertisement of "La Boheme." When we went inside, Josette started singing the aria, "Mi Chiamano Mimi." There, on the stage, covered with the peasant's coat and girded with his belt, stood the cow. "She is only four years old," said the man, her former owner, "and not accustomed to bombs and artillery. She is a little nervous, so I brought her here."

We called her Mimi, and led her to our garden, where she had beautiful roses to eat, and straw from the packing of some bottles. Mimi gave much milk, which we gave to the more seriously wounded. We could not have kept her in the theater, because the theater was burned down that night.

Since we had nowhere to place all of the casualties, I went with the commandant and Dominik in search of suitable buildings, one for a military hospital, the other for a civilian one. For the latter we decided on a government building not far from Maltanski.

For the military hospital, we had to choose between three buildings; one was an annex of the Royal Castle, where the Castle guards were quartered, and we went to see it.

On our way we saw a crowd of breathless men running. What could be the matter? We were told that President

Starzynski had announced that he needed 600 men to take up arms immediately. Later we met men who were disconsolate because they had not arrived in time; those who lived nearer the rallying place had gotten there first.

Arriving at the Royal Castle, we found it badly damaged; shells were whistling around. I would have preferred to keep close to the walls, but Dominik and Stas went right through the middle of the courtyard as if nothing was the matter, so there was no alternative but to stiffen my neck muscles and go with them.

The Royal Castle was the official residence of the President of Poland. After World War I it had been carefully restored, and it housed innumerable treasures—paintings and furnishings. Mr. Brokl, the custodian, was a bachelor who had devoted his life and love to the Royal Castle. He told us how he had tried to protect the historic relics, taking them to the cellar.

From the Royal Castle we went to see the third possible location for the hospital, and then returned to Maltanski.

We wanted to consult the full executive council before moving ahead. In the meantime we designated Mrs. Stanislawa Tarnowska as director of nursing of our second military hospital. She was courageous and a good organizer; she knew how to make people calm and confident.

She had come to us on September 8, during the afternoon Maltanski was bombed. Entering the hall, she had asked, "Can I be of use? I am a nurse." "Yes," I had answered. She had opened her suitcase, taken out a white uniform, and said, "I am ready; where shall I go?" I had told her, "Number five ward." "Thank you," she had said, and went there. From then on she kept that ward, the largest and the most exposed of the wards, as calm and peaceful as possible.

The task of a ward nurse was not an easy one. Though every ward was full—two wounded in each bed, at any moment it might receive, without warning, twenty or fifty more.

Mrs. Tarnowska, in her new function, would have to count on her own resourcefulness, as once the hospital was set up we would not be able to give her much help. The new hospital would be for the less seriously wounded, and it would have no resident physician, only a visiting physician from Maltanski. To make her task easier, she would have eight Boy Scouts, brave and resourceful, to assist her, and she was given her choice from among the nurses and nursing aides.

Cigarettes became very scarce; we could not give more than five a day to a wounded person, and we ourselves smoked an awful mixture—home-grown tobacco mixed with the cuttings of cigars and something that looked very much like hay.

That day in the city I noticed places where a soldier could stop, sit down, and have his feet washed and his socks changed in nearly every street. Warsaw women were giving this service on their own initiative as a simple, humble contribution to the work of the weary soldiers, defenders of Warsaw. It was touching and comforting to soldiers suffering from painfully swollen feet who had marched hundreds of miles, day and night with little rest, to reach the capital. This deed of mercy was done by society women as well as poor women.

In the afternoon, a number of wounded were brought out of the Royal Castle. All except one, however, died in the ambulances, and the one who reached the hospital alive died at the entrance of the operating theater. The poor young boy —he had wanted so much to live. As he was lifted from the ambulance he asked me, "Will I live?" I was surprised that he asked such a question, because there seemed so much life in him. Yet a moment later he collapsed from an internal hemorrhage. He was the last survivor of the Castle guard.

In the area of the Royal Castle there was no hospital, and the wounded had to be carried a long distance on stretchers. Since many were dying from loss of blood on the way to Maltanski, we wanted to open a hospital there. We decided to give the Royal Castle another look, and we thought that Mrs. Tarnowska should go with us to see how she felt about assuming responsibility there.

Entering by the side gate, we noticed on the small lawn a fresh grave, which had not been there that morning. It was the grave of Mr. Brokl, the custodian, who had been killed during the midday bombing. He had died in this Royal Castle, which he had loved, and whose relics he had been trying to save.

Those past few hours had made a great difference in the condition of the Royal Castle, but, thank God, it had so far escaped fire. The annex, which we had considered as a possible place for the hospital, was almost rubble.

As the Castle was so badly damaged, we decided to take a nearby government building instead for our second military hospital. Mrs. Tarnowska stayed there. We told her that we would supply her with whatever she needed as it was necessary to open the new hospital the next day. After we moved the less seriously wounded and the convalescents there it would give us much more room in Maltanski. Mrs. Tarnowska knew that she could not expect to have a surgeon, because there were so few. Those we had were already overworked, and senior medical students were attending surgical patients, often performing serious operations.

A real catastrophe befell us before evening—the water supply failed. As it appeared that the stoppage was only in our area, we hoped it would be only temporary. We had filled every possible receptacle with water, but that was hardly enough for a few hours.

Saturday, September 16, 1939

The adjustments that the hospital's professional staff had to make were difficult. Procedures they had been taught in medical or nursing school, such as using X-rays to find the exact location of a bullet imbedded in a bone, or to estimate the scatter of shrapnel splinters or the extent of the area rammed by particles from an explosive bullet, were out of the question. Surgical instruments were blunt; a broken thermometer or syringe could not be replaced.

The greatest danger and the ward staff's greatest responsibility was the constant threat of panic, for if panic were to seize one ward it could spread through the whole hospital. The toll in lives in a stampede might be enormous. The staff members in charge of caring for the wounded were senior medical students and "nurses" with a few days of first-aid training. Graduate doctors and registered nurses did surgery, decided on admissions, served in out-patient clinics, and supervised the emergency medical and nursing staff.

Until the evening of the fifteenth we had water. Then it failed. A hospital with about a thousand people without water! The steam boilers in the kitchen burst. Interrupting an executive meeting, the chef rushed in the office, all upset, to say that he would not be able to cook. The commandant looked at him and said, "Oh, how dreadful, chef Kwiecinski! What, may I ask, did you plan to cook?" The chef's eyes bulged. Everyone laughed, for there was nothing to cook. We had only some bread, which we received each day from the Red Cross.

A hospital without water! Surgical instruments and dressings could no longer be sterilized. All sanitary arrangements were disrupted.

In the yard of an ancient house a few blocks away someone discovered a well. But as we were not the only ones using it, we feared that it would soon run dry. Water for the hospital had to be carried, and we had only a few pails. The carriers had to cross the square, and some were killed performing this task. Water became so precious that it had to be rationed and used for drinking only.

At this time, with the water supply cut off, the Germans introduced a new weapon—the incendiary bomb.

That day the colonel was a proud man. When he had volunteered his services, we did not know what he would be able to do. He seemed so old, as if he were a mummy. In the Russo-Japanese war, he had been a colonel in charge of a medical unit in Siberia and had been taken prisoner in the battle of Port Arthur, in 1905. Since his retirement he had lived for many years in the suburbs of Warsaw, growing mulberry trees and cultivating silkworms. At first, the young doctors did not have much respect for him because he was completely unaware of the newest medical thinking and because he was preoccupied with the fate of his silkworms, which were already behind the enemy lines. As the days went on, however, they recognized that his experience with primitive conditions and his resourcefulness complemented their skills. On the day the water supply was cut off, he was besieged for advice on what could be done. His 1905 methods proved most applicable.

In the morning the bombing and shelling came as usual, but our work had to go on. Everyone on our staff could be counted on. Everyone felt that the simplest thing one did contributed to the same great cause.

Bombing, which continued for several hours at a stretch three or four times a day, was mainly responsible for the destruction of buildings. Artillery shelling, however, killed more people and caused more fires.

At first most of the staff had slept under their own roofs, but day by day, many who found their homes in ruins had returned to the hospital for shelter. We were so convinced nothing could happen to this particular hospital that people felt safe there.

When members of the staff went to see their families, they usually found them hidden in dark, damp cellars. On the way they had to hop from one gateway to another and run close to the walls to avoid being shelled, or spotted by planes, which flew just above the housetops and machine-gunned people. The staff members saw much misery about which they could do nothing, and in the streets they felt like tracked game. They were happy when they returned to the hospital.

At noon a message came from headquarters asking us to go to the Red Cross depot to remove drugs and surgical instruments that hospitals needed badly. This depot was in no man's land between the defenders and the enemy. Even of us—the commandant, Mrs. Glinski, a doctor, three guards, and I—took a truck and the Fiat and started for the depot. The worst part of our journey was passing a cemetery that had been shelled ever since morning. Many graves had been demolished. A dead man in full dress was hanging across the wall; pieces of bodies were everywhere. The stench was terrific all over the town, but in this particular spot it was beyond words.

After passing the cemetery and an open space, we reached the railway track and then the Red Cross depot. We could see the Germans entrenched not far away, behind tanks that had run out of gasoline. It was quieter here—the shells whistled, but the machine guns waited.

We parked the vehicles in a sheltered place and began to work. By now we were skilled enough to jump quickly between storehouses to avoid machine-gun fire. But it was not so easy when we were carrying things. After the truck was loaded I decided that I would take it to the hospital. I told the staff members that if the shell fire intensified they were to take shelter and I would find them on my return. The danger was that the Germans would realize that we were only a handful of people and attack us. We had only four rifles among us.

On my way back I found that the hospital neighborhood had been heavily shelled. That morning a battery had been installed in the vicinity of our hospital and had fired on the enemy. The German batteries were returning the fire in an effort to silence ours, and Maltanski was in the line of fire. I was in a hurry, but we could advance only slowly because the street was obstructed. At the square, a crowd was running in panic. I stopped the truck to let them pass. At that moment a bomb dropped on the pavement; it stood upright and then exploded. I had not heard the plane. I had seen bombs dropping from a plane's belly before, but only this time did I see a bomb touch the ground and then explode. A number of people fell down like bags of sand; the rest vanished. The driver and I jumped out of the truck to see if we could help, but they had all been killed outright.

We passed by, and just as we arrived at the front of the hospital we heard a loud detonation inside the building. My first concern was that panic would seize the hospital, but as I went toward the wing where the explosion had occurred it was clear that there was no panic. A heavy artillery shell had burst in number five ward, where women and children were lying. Smoke and white dust filled the passage; women shrieked.

Monsignor Dobiecki was standing at the door of the ward, blood running down his forehead, his head and cassock white with plaster and dust. His calm and forceful voice rose above all other sounds: "Silence, let us ask God's help." Both young nurses assigned to the ward, though covered with debris, were hard at work. Fortunately, there were not many casualties. The chaplain had been in the ward, giving the last sacraments to a dying woman, while the artillery fire was coming closer and closer. When the neighboring building had been destroyed and a shell had struck the gable of the hospital, he had ordered the evacuation of the ward to the corridor. It was owing to this decision that so many escaped.

The wall of the operating theater was demolished, and the operating table was upset, but nobody was hurt. In clouds of dust one could see doctors operating on a patient on the floor.

A patient leaving the hospital had just been stepping onto the pavement when a blast had injured him severely. He had to be picked up and returned to his bed in the ward.

It was clear that the operating theater and number five ward had to be written off. Also, the planks that we had nailed up the day before to replace broken windows had all been blown out. And so it went; work finished was constantly destroyed and had to be redone.

The situation in the hospital was well in hand, and the shelling seemed to have quieted down. I at once started for the depot, as the people I had left there were in danger. We had not gone far when a burst of shrapnel slightly damaged the truck. We still could drive on, however. It was important for us to bring back our people, as well as the drugs and instruments. As we passed opposite a railroad station, another bomb exploded, and that time the poor truck seemed finished. It hobbled along so slowly that I got out and hurried back to the hospital on foot. When I got there, Zwerdling had returned with the Buick, so I started out again.

On the way we met the commandant, returning in the loaded Fiat. He stood on the running board, clutching the frame of the car with one hand, and with the other holding a wounded person whom he had picked up on the road. I told him about the explosion in the hospital; he told me that the situation in the Red Cross depot had worsened, and that our staff members were in the shelter, awaiting my arrival.

I found that artillery was now shelling the depot directly.

It would be unthinkable to drive the car through the firing, so we sheltered it in a niche in the cemetery wall. I had to go on alone. I was afraid. The shells were very small, but they came like hornets, seventeen a minute—I counted them by my watch.

If I could manage to get to the railroad track all would be well; but to do so I would have to cross 100 yards of open field. I took a deep breath and dashed across, and fell beside the tracks. My heart beat so hard that it seemed louder than the bursts of the shells. I rested for a moment and then jumped across the tracks, falling into a ditch on the other side. Now only a few yards remained to the depot. I set out again . . . I felt a terrible blow on my head. All was darkness.

A few hours later consciousness returned to me like a sudden wakening from a dream. I observed that I was holding a glass of wine, that my helmet was broken and had three bullet marks, and that blood was running from my ear. I had no idea what had happened in those few hours. I was told that I had got up and walked to the shelter where it had been arranged that the staff members would be waiting, told them to follow me, and to everybody's amazement walked back to the car without any rush or concern for the shelling. My behavior had seemed strange to the staff, especially when they asked me a question and did not receive a reply. Subconscious motivation had taken over and made me perform like a wound-up clock.

We had to have an operating theater somewhere, for more and more wounded kept coming in. Dominik, the commandant, and I went to look for a suitable place. We decided on a bank half a block away. It had four floors, a big hall with a glass cupola, and thick walls. We could place patients on the first floor, which would be safer than the upper floors. The main consideration was that the operating theater should be safe, and that operations would not have to be finished on the floor. The basement, we thought, and the vaults would just serve the purpose. The lack of water made preparing the operating theater difficult.

In Maltanski, when there was some extra work to be done, the messenger boys went and told staff members who were resting in relatively safe places. The kitchen and the entrance hall were such places and there were a few other spots sheltered from shrapnel. Whoever could, came to give a hand preparing the new operating theater. The commandant had to leave, but Dominik and I remained and Monsignor Dobiecki joined us, as did chef Kwiecinski with a few members of his staff, Senator Szymanski, and some guards with Corporal Uptas.

The bank vaults were in the basement. A few steps down from the main entrance was one long room, probably ten feet by forty, which we planned to use as the operating theater. There were also two small rooms connected by doors, where supplies could be stored.

In the room for the operating theater the windows were very high and narrow. They had no glass; at this time it was most unlikely that there was a single unshattered glass pane in Warsaw. Uptas and his men made air holes in each window frame, using bricks, and then filled in rubble and sand around the bricks. There was no light, but there was fresh air, and shrapnel splinters could not enter and ricochet from the walls. We emptied the vaults of boxes, piles of documents, and books; swept the area; and then, as a finishing touch washed it, using one pail of water with lysol.

Senator Szymanski, as chief physician, was indispensable in advising what was needed for the operating theater. We had only one operating table, and, wondering where we could find a second one, called Jacek Goldman, who worked for us as a driver and a supplier of blood donors. Goldman used to be a co-owner of a pawnshop, and he knew the city well. We hoped that he could find an operating table, and so we sent him treasure-hunting with Roman, who as assistant to the commandant had authority to requisition whatever the hospital needed (the owner would be reimbursed by the city government). Before ten in the evening the operating theater had two tables.

Each day, after the air raid started, we expected an increased number of wounded. Casualties from the artillery shelling, however, came in a steady flow. In normal times the bank's large hall might have made a good waiting room, but in wartime it was not safe, for bits of shrapnel rained through the open roof. The vestibule, however, was wide and protected, and patients on stretchers waiting their turn in the operating theater would be safe there. If the vestibule became overcrowded the stretchers would have to be sheltered inside the gateways of adjoining houses, which by then had been demolished.

When the operating theater began to function I returned to Maltanski. Soon afterward the artillery fire grew stronger and stronger. It clearly was focusing on our area, for shells were bursting all around. There seemed little chance that the hospital would last out the night. The annex was hit by three shells in its back wall. The planks that had been nailed over the glassless windows throughout the hospital that morning were blown out. We had no candles or lanterns, but the glow from the burning city provided light. Faces seemed red, and dark shadows made the already frightening scene appear even more ghastly. Bits of shrapnel were freely ricocheting off the walls.

The wounded could hear the crash of collapsing houses, could feel the danger mounting. Standing in the hall, as I was, one could feel tension in the very walls of the hospital. At any moment panic could seize the wards. It was important for us to support the ward staff. Dominik, the commandant, Mon-

signor Dobiecki, Mrs. Glinski, Josette, and I separated to go
to those wards that were in the greatest danger. Ward number
four became my responsibility. Going up the wide marble
stairs like an automaton, my feet felt like lead. There was not
a particle of me that was not frightened. As explosions echoed
in the big hall, the gentle tinkling of the Venetian crystal
chandeliers irritated me with their inappropriate sweetness.
To reach ward number four it was necessary to cross number
four A. It was not really a ward, but a part of the hallway
leading to a ballroom. It had two niches. We had squeezed
six beds into this place and put two wounded in each of them.
For this "ward" we could not spare a doctor or a nurse. Sergeant Grooshka, who was in charge, slept in an easy chair.
His fracture and the contraption built around his body required a special adjustment in a bed; but we could not supply
a bed, so an easy chair had to substitute. The men in the ward
had fractures that had been attended to on admission, and we
could do no more than provide them with half of a bed. One
of the men was a German.

I usually took a detour to avoid going through ward number
four A, because each time I stepped in, even if I had been
there only a few minutes before, Sergeant Grooshka would
jump up, salute, shout "Attention," and insist that every man
stretch out in his bed, and look straight at me. (In the army
regulations my rank required "honoring.") He then would
say: "Sergeant Grooshka reporting. Ward number four A,
six beds, twelve wounded, nothing has happened." When it
was in an emergency that I went through ward number four
A, such foolishness was irritating. But the sergeant was within
his rights; I had to submit, but did so ungraciously.

When next entering ward number four A, I held myself
stiffly erect. Then came "Attention," and Sergeant Grooshka
stood saluting in front of me. He recited the usual formula.
I was not impatient or annoyed, but desperately weary. Is this
necessary, I thought, at such a time? Suddenly I understood;

it came in a flash. This man, himself in constant pain, took responsibility for these wounded, one of whom was a German, an enemy, who only a few days before was helping to destroy the city, and trying to kill as many of us as he could. There was never trouble in that ward. When Sergeant Grooshka finished his recitation with the usual "nothing has happened," I understood that it was because of his strength and devotion to duty that nothing did happen. I realized that I had never given him recognition or support. Sergeant Grooshka must have sensed that I understood, for he whispered, half to himself and half to me, "Perhaps nothing will happen."

I told him that it must have been sad for him each time I rushed through with barely enough time to receive his report, but that we understood his contribution and were counting on him that night to see that nothing happened and that the prisoner would be protected. I promised to inspect his ward the next day.

When I entered the next ward, number four, I had my mask on again and tried to smile. The door creaked. In the ward reigned a nervous, heavy silence, but electricity was in the air. Over 400 pairs of eyes looked at me. Something had to be done. If this tension should explode, nothing could control it. Ants were running down my backbone, and I had to set my chattering teeth. I wanted to run away and hide myself underground. At first I tried a cheap trick, and asked why the door creaked, since I had asked the day before that the door hinges be greased. There was enough noise without this abominable creaking, I added. A less seriously wounded soldier, that day's orderly, went to attend to the door. I went to the medicine cupboard—nothing to say about that. Hundreds of ideas were whizzing in my head as to what could be done to help in this painful crisis. The orderly reported that the door was no longer creaking.

My mask of warriors came off; it would fool no one anyway. The Maltese cross on my uniform, the emblem of my function, became real to me with all it represented. I said that each of us knew what danger we were in, and that that was why I came to be with them at this time. Then a truly brilliant idea came to me. A few days before, I had brought from the customhouse some barrels of superb Chablis, which were now in the cellars of the hospital. I said that if we had to appear before our Saviour before the night was over, He would not mind, I was sure, if we had enjoyed a little merriment, so we might as well have some wine. "Wine! Wine! Wine!" shot throughout the wards. The barrels were opened, and the wine was carried in pails through the wards. For days we had had so little food that it took very little wine to make the hospital gay.

We did not hear the shells bursting, or the houses crashing around the hospital. We could not have cared less if we were to have been killed at any moment. I went around the wards and finally to the kitchen, where the drivers, guards, and stretcher-bearers were gathered, having their little drink. My driver, Jacob Zwerdling, was making a speech. Zwerdling's past was eventful, but it had not been gladly tolerated by society. I strongly suspected that he came to us from a reformatory, for at the beginning of the siege the prisons had been opened. Zwerdling was short and bow-legged, and had but one tooth. He always wore handmade shoes, a yellow plush coat, a red muffler, a steel helmet, and a gas mask over his shoulder. He spoke with a guttural Jewish accent. Zwerdling insisted on everyone's recognizing that he was by no means an unimportant person. He would have his audience know that he had lived in Monte Carlo, and had had a chauffeur-driven car. When a Pole was unlucky in the casino, whom would he go to for help? To the consulate? No, to Zwerdling. He was the one who would lend him money; he was the one to see for an evening with the most beautiful ladies on the Riviera. "And I always thought that I was a coward," Zwerdling concluded, "I am a—hero!"

After midnight came a telephone call from our liaison officer at headquarters. Taking the receiver, I heard an onslaught of anxious queries. "Are you still alive? Is there no panic? Would you like me to come and help you?" Each of us wondered if the other was mad, for instead of talking of death, I told him, "We are singing. Are you deaf?" And, "Why do you do not hear the music? Do you want to come and join us, and enjoy life as we are doing?" At that moment the telephone exchange was completely destroyed. Shortly afterward the liaison officer rushed in, and, true to our promise, was met with a glass of wine. He stayed in the hospital till morning, not because he was needed but because he could not walk straight.

Sunday, September 17, 1939

Sunday, the day of rest, began with a heavy bombardment. Bad news came from the city. A part of the Royal Castle had been destroyed. Fires were burning in the Sejm (the parliament building). The vaults of St. John's Cathedral had collapsed as the High Mass was being celebrated, with the church full of people. It seemed as if every third house was in flames. Unceasingly we heard over the radio calls to the inhabitants to help put fires out at specified places.

The newspapers were appearing no longer. They had been publishing only one-page editions, but they were a symbol of civilization, a link with a world of which we were a part and from which we felt cut off. Our newspaper was replaced by a mimeographed bulletin. It was valuable to have that much; nevertheless, the change made me feel pain. One of the components of the defense of Warsaw had crumbled. It seemed that the disappearance of that piece of paper, with its inaccurate information, made us feel more desolate than the disappearance of our planes from the battlefield in the sky.

The wind whistled through the hospital; we had to nail up planks again. I wondered how long they would stay this time? It is true that the planks protected us from the wind and from bomb and shrapnel splinters. Also, the nights were cool, and the boarded-up windows offered some protection against the chill. On the other hand, to have the wards half darkened during the day was depressing for everyone.

Monsignor Dobiecki had arranged a little chapel in a room upstairs. It was too dangerous to have a ward there. But Monsignor said he was certain our Lord did not mind being exposed to danger, and if anyone wished to kep Him company it was a personal matter in which we should not interfere. That morning a number of those who were able to drag themselves to mount two flights of stairs went to participate in the Sunday Mass. A bomb burst so near that the blast threw the people down as they stood to sing the national anthem. No one, however, was injured.

When Maltanski first opened, it had been safe to be out after an air raid had ended. But once artillery fire had started there was no more safety. There seemed to be two patterns of directing artillery fire: concentrating on one area or one object, and scattering the fire all over. Both patterns seemed to be operating at the same time. One never knew from which direction a shell would come; it would come without warning and seemingly without purpose.

Monsignor Dobiecki had installed the chapel the day he became our chaplain, and had made Zdzis, the nine-year-old son of our secretary, Mrs. Sicinski, his choir boy. We were grateful to Monsignor for his choice, for Zdzis was such a lively boy that he was constantly where he was not supposed to be. Mrs. Sicinski was already having trouble with her seven-year-old Grazynka, who did not want to spend her days in the dark wine cellar. It was difficult for a mother to handle two living pieces of quicksilver.

We asked Monsignor to keep an eye on Zdzis and give him as many tasks as possible. We solved the problem with Grazynka by making her responsible for Poos, a small, white, shaggy, four-month-old puppy.

Poos had come to our hospital as if it was his own home, made a mess in the middle of the entrance hall, and then trotted away to seek children—straight to the cellar. He was very happy and began at once to have a party with the children, who named him Poos. Poos was carefree, unafraid of the bombing, and played joyfully in front of the hospital. We recognized the value of having some creature give pleasure to children and take them into their own child's world, as our adult world was so terrible, especially where we were. Members of the staff shared their bread rations with the puppy. Every time Poos wanted to do his business, he interrupted his game in the square and came running into the hall, to the despair of those who had to keep the hospital clean. We made Grazynka personally responsible for the safety and good manners of Poos, and that kept her fully occupied.

I went to see President Starzynski to ask whether it was possible to hurry the repair of the water main. He realized only too well that our waterless hospital was in a desperate position, and he promised to send additional work teams and to do whatever else he could. On his word one could rely.

Yet another example of gallantry on the part of one of our staff came from driver Kowalski. While I was in conference with President Starzynski the shelling was intense, and I was worried about our car, which had been left around the corner. I was certain the car would be destroyed, but I did not worry much about the driver, because there was a shelter at the entrance of the building. When it was time for me to leave, he was not at the entrance, and when I glanced into the street

I realized to my horror that Kowalski had remained in the car, with the engine running, to be ready to rush me from the shelled quarter as soon as I appeared.

That day Roman, assistant to the commandant, was annoyed. He complained that he was getting all the dirty work to do. His anger was directed toward the Girl Guides, and he was threatening that if they appeared in Maltanski, he would teach them a lesson they would never forget as long as they lived. When Dominik commented that they might not live very long, Roman did not feel any better. But we had some coffee and wine, and that cheered him up.

His trouble involved the exchange of wounded between hospitals had developed in the city. A wounded person was always carried to the nearest place where there was a doctor or a nurse, and from there to a hospital. Many auxiliary hospitals had been set up during the siege, and there were a number of first-aid posts. None of those facilities had operating theaters and therefore could not accept the more seriously wounded.

The hospitals were overcrowded, so overcrowded that after an operation the patient would be left lying on a stretcher, waiting for half of a bed. No hospital at that time could provide a bed to each patient. Some had to lie on the floor between beds, in corridors, on staircase landings, or in passageways.

Hospitals with operating theaters were accepting one seriously wounded patient in exchange for two or more slightly wounded from auxiliary hospitals.

That morning Roman had taken two of our patients to the well-equipped city hospital, which was like a town in itself. One of the patients he wanted to transfer to the city hospital was a woman whose case had no connection with the war. A paraffin lamp had burst, setting her dress on fire and causing third-degree burns. It was not possible to keep her in any of our wards because of the terrible odor of her rotting flesh, which attracted all the flies in the area.

The second patient was a wounded soldier suffering from scabies. We had no quarantine ward, so it was impossible to nurse him without great risk to the other patients.

Roman felt that those two people should have been accepted without our having to take eight seriously wounded in exchange. He was most indignant because when he had arrived with our two patients, the Girl Guides were bringing theirs, and they "spoiled the market." He had had to exchange the woman for six seriously wounded patients, and the soldier for two.

One of our nurses went home for half a day, and rumor circulated around the hospital that she had eaten potatoes. Everyone was envious.

We still had bread, horsemeat which had to be used sparingly, tea and cocoa from the customhouse, and a few lentils from the Red Cross. We had no potatoes or other vegetables. For breakfast we had tea without sugar or cream and a little bread, but so tiny a piece that it would disappear in two bites. At noon, we had horsemeat soup, with some lentils in it; for supper, cocoa made with hot water, without sugar or milk.

In the evening, water reappeared! What a boon! Everything was washed; that night we were like one big laundry. Before dawn, after the operating theater had finished its work, it was beautifully cleaned too. But utilities that we had taken for granted before could not be taken for granted any longer. We had to make the best of everything while it lasted.

I was to go to headquarters to report on the functioning and available room of our hospitals and to suggest where to direct convoys of wounded in case we could not accept them. There was still time, so I suggested to Josette that we go see how the kitchen staff was getting along, and what supplies we had for the next day. On a side table were piled some loaves of bread. My heart contracted when I realized that it was all we had for over 1000 people. Some containers of lentils and sugar were on hand, so the cocoa for the evening meal apparently would have some sugar. Red candies were lying on top of the sugar. Josette tasted a few and found them very good. I asked what the candies were. "Well," said Chef Kwiecinski, "this afternoon, when our staff was bringing a bag of sugar from the Red Cross, a horse was killed and they took the meat. As they put the meat on top of the bag, some blood soaked into the sugar. It is fresh, so I will use this sugar for cocoa for the most seriously wounded. It is very fortifying." "Excellent! Excellent!" said Josette, but shot out of the kitchen. It was time to leave for headquarters, but I could not find Josette, and went alone. I suspected, however, that the candies were something less than "excellent."

When I was going through the hall later that night I saw a soldier dragging a wounded comrade. As the nurse helped the wounded man to the operating theater, the other soldier sat down and asked for a glass of water. A jug of water was always available in the hall, but during the time it took to fill the glass the man fell fast asleep, his helmet on his head and his rifle in his hands. Carefully I unbuckled his helmet and took away the gun. Next day, at noon, he suddenly jumped up, and at first did not know where he was, or how he had gotten there.

Under my bed every morning was an arsenal, as I received all the wounded who were brought in during the night, and did not want to waken Roman, who was in charge of the weapon storeroom. I only called him when I had hand grenades. I had a great respect for this mysterious weapon. I did not know how to handle it, and preferred to treat it with due consideration and at a distance.

All of us were very tired, for we had so little rest. Before the attack we had had many illusions concerning personal needs. I had imagined, for instance, that I needed to sleep ten hours a day, but in wartime if I snatched two hours in install-ments I considered myself rich.

Monday, September 18, 1939

In the early morning the Germans dropped leaflets, saying:

WARSAW HAS SURRENDERED!
The Polish Government has run away.
Lay down arms.
Surrender, because otherwise we shall be forced to bomb you with air force and artillery!

Since the Germans had not waited until then to bomb us, the leaflets did not have the effect the authors wished. They stiffened our spirit, and the bad spelling amused us.

At noon news spread that the Soviet army had crossed the Polish frontier the day before and was advancing along the entire front. We were confused and bewildered, and really did not believe it.

We clung to the belief that our allies would soon send us help through Romania. There were no signs our determina-tion had weakened.

That morning one of our wounded patients, Klos, died. We had tried hard to save him. He was a soldier who had been sent on patrol. Returning at daybreak to his unit in a village, he had heard voices and hid in a ditch. A detachment of Germans passed, and Klos, thinking himself safe, got up, but they saw him, caught him, and disarmed him. An officer who spoke Polish fluently questioned him: "Where do you come from?" Silence. "Are the Polish troops still in this village?" Silence. At that moment a Polish cavalry squadron could be seen leaving the village. "You are free, Polish swine, be off!" Klos turned away, but had not gone four steps when the officer shot him with an explosive bullet. Most persons hit in the trunk by an explosive bullet do not live to be brought to a hospital, as such a bullet ravages an area of about eight inches in diameter. It was amazing that a German officer, at such short range, should have missed his mark—and because of this the incident became known, for Klos was hit only in the thigh.

The German detachment proceeded on its way. Klos lay two days without any assistance. At first he lay on the side of the road. Then, as his body was interfering with traffic, some German soldiers threw him into the ditch.

Some women of the village found him, and in the night smuggled him to Warsaw and brought him to our hospital.

The doctor told me, "It is only his youth and the prayers of his mother in some village that can save him, because gangrene has already set it."

Going through the wards on the night when he was admitted, I noticed that he was not asleep. "Why are you not sleeping? Are you suffering much? Would you like anything?" "Yes, madam, I suffer, but I am so happy to be on Polish ground again, to have a bed to lie on, with clean linen, to have something to eat, and to be among people who care, that I do not want to sleep, because I want to enjoy it."

He was weakening fast. An artery burst—it had been plugged—and he was given a blood transfusion. Shortly afterward another artery burst, and again he was given a transfusion.

He never uttered a complaint, and was always grateful for everything. The previous night he had been so weak that we thought he would not live till morning. He asked for a priest, and Monsignor Dobiecki came at five A.M. with the Holy Viaticum. I was with the nurse attending him. At seven o'clock he tried to whisper, and I bent to catch the words, thinking he wanted something. He said, "You have had no breakfast today because of me."

I went out, because I did not want the others in the ward to see that I was crying. But on the way to my office I felt that I was failing him and was a deserter. For the sake of the mask of warriors, which requires action with no display of feeling, I had forsaken him, and in him, all humanity. I felt that my duty was to be with Klos when he died.

So I went back to the ward. The feeling of security of one of our wounded patients depended on his trust in my judgment to provide safety and to see that he had what he needed; but it mainly depended on the belief that I would not desert him in need.

My uniform, with the Cross of Malta, was the symbol indicating that I represented the values of humanity, which go beyond providing physical care. I had to represent humanity when its values needed to be asserted. I did not want Klos to die; it was monstrous that we were losing the battle for his life. It was a tragedy that he had to suffer and die in a hospital ward, away from those who loved him. At the time a human being needs help most, he so often is left alone. I resolved that although we would lose the fight for his life, Klos and all who needed understanding and compassion would receive it as if they were surrounded by their own families. When I came back his eyes were bluer, and very quietly and modestly he died.

I felt tired and went into our garden to get some rest and regain my balance. It seemed not to be the same garden into which I had stepped on the morning of the seventh; war had reached it. The roses had been eaten by Mimi, the cow, and

there were crosses to mark graves. At first they had been individual graves, but now we could no longer afford this
luxury for our dead, and buried them in common graves.

Mimi hurried to me and pressed her head against me. I laid
my hands on her neck and horns, and she seemed to feel much
happier. Poor creature, I thought, you were afraid to be alone
too, the other day when you tried to force your way into the
ward through the French window. Perhaps we will think of
something that will make your lot easier. You are much thin-
ner, yet you give the same amount of milk, and we need it so
much. You know it goes for the most seriously wounded and
for the smallest children. Klos, to whom we gave a little of
your milk every day, died this morning. Tomorrow he will be
here in a grave, for we will dig a grave for those who died in
the past twenty-four hours before the first raid.

Behind the operating theater in the vault of the bank was a
windowless strong-room. We decided to use it as shelter for
the smallest children, those who were too young to run
around. The evening before, I had brought my sister with
her children and placed them there. She had had difficulty in
controlling her fear, but here she felt safe and could look
after other small children, who had been picked up from
various places. Having much time on her hands, she could get
them to tell her their names, so we could find out where they
belonged and locate their kin.

At the beginning of the siege, there had been a common
supply depot for all the hospitals. Everyone tried to build up
an individual store for his particular hospital. I recalled the
scene in the customhouse, when I had given the Red Cross
half of the crates of raisins to which I had a claim as discoverer,
in exchange for information on where cocoa could be found.
At this later time our concern was that all the wounded would
have whatever was available. We had discarded the pettiness

of competition. We shared. We did not store things that we might need the next day when there was a hospital or first-aid post that was in need that day.

When supplies were centered in a depot, more than once they were destroyed. Also some hospital staffs could not reach the place. Each day we were notified where bread was to be collected and where dressings were available. A responsible person from a hospital would be sent to collect whatever was needed, using his or her own judgment, and make out the usual requisition forms.

That day our daily ration of bread had to be collected from an auxiliary depot. Upon arrival we found the doorway blocked by the bodies of two dead men. We were in a great hurry, for it was midday and the wounded in Maltanski had not yet had anything to eat. We had to move the bodies. The driver seized one by the feet, and cursing in fury, dragged it out of our way. "Jan Kowalski," I said, "We are in a rush, but those are human bodies. You and I may be blocking this door or another one at any time; you would not like to be removed that way yourself." Jan was not a sophisticated man, but he understood that he had failed in human feelings, and how easy it was to do so, just as I had understood it when a man hit by a shell was in my way during the episode of the chestnut horses.

On entering the building, how disappointed we were to find it empty and completely destroyed inside! Where was the bread? Again time had been wasted.

We found our rations in a near-by high school, which had been converted into an auxiliary hospital. Artillery had heavily shelled this area, but two buildings next to the school, a museum and an Evangelical church, protected it a little, although both were already greatly damaged. As we were loading the bread, two shells hit the roof and a third fell in the courtyard, right on a barrel of gasoline. A loud explosion followed, and dirty smoke covered everything in an instant.

The hospital was gripped by panic. There were shrieks, and in the twinkling of an eye the staircase was blocked by the wounded men, trampling on one another, while others jumped from the second- and third-floor windows, breaking their limbs, some killing themselves.

When this happened, I was standing outside with Jan and my driver, and two of our men were throwing bags of bread from the fourth floor, where it had been stored. We quickly loaded the truck.

I realized at once that there was more noise and smoke than danger, for our men on the fourth floor would have no difficulty in quickly extinguishing the fire. But the panic had to be quelled, or many more would be trampled to death.

I leaped into the hall, and drew out my gun. The hall was empty, but the rolling mass of intermingled bodies almost reached the landing. "Stop," I cried, and I fired over their heads. "It's over; return to the wards." Doctors operating in a classroom on the left of the hall, and the clerical staff, working in another classroom, were not aware of what had happened until they heard the shot. Then they rushed out into the hall.

Patients lying on the street and those on the staircase had to be taken back to the wards. I sent the bread to Maltanski and remained with two men to give a hand in this emergency.

Someone took the other end of my stretcher, and we began to carry in the patients. Having finished the work, we put away the stretcher, and then I recognized my partner— Count Michel Komorowski, chairman of the Horse Racing Association. He had happened to be passing; I had happened to be there.

I invited him to come over to Maltanski for a cup of black coffee and a glass of wine. I felt we deserved it. While we waited for the truck that had taken the bread to the hospital, we sat on the steps of the school to rest. Opposite us, Kronenberg Palace was burning. It was burning marvelously, more beautifully than were the surrounding buildings. It burned calmly, surely, without hurry, enveloped in flames from basement to roof—nobody disturbed the fire. When I passed by that night it was still aflame.

By evening Dominik had not yet returned. The bombing and artillery fire were heavier than usual, so we were most anxious about him. Suddenly he rushed into the hospital with a joyful shout: "I escaped them! And I've bought another cow! A lively creature! I had to lead her on a string through the town—a better show than Barnum & Bailey could ever put up!" We all regretted we had missed it. Mimi, I was certain, would be very happy, and would not moo desperately during the next bombing, for she would have company.

Later, I was looking for Mrs. Glinski; she seemed to have disappeared. Finally I found her, attending to Monsignor Dobiecki's head wound. He had been cut in several places two days before, when ward number five had been struck. Although Monsignor was a diabetic, he had refused to have dressings done in the daytime, because the other patients would see it, which he felt would not be good for their morale. He knew that late in the evening Mrs. Glinski could dress his wounds without anyone's knowing it. I could not have known about it, except by accident.

Late at night, when we had some time, we talked about the Soviet Army's advance into Poland. But where were they headed to? We knew that it all meant something serious, but what? Did they come as our allies or our enemies? Roman was working at our radio, trying to get a station in the eastern part of Poland. When he got it, a speaker was giving a long talk about the Soviet Army's having come to liberate people from the capitalistic "bloodsuckers." "And now," the voice said, "we will have Shoora tell how she feels about being liberated." Shoora was introduced as a Jewish widow with several children, living in a small town. "And now, Shoora, tell in your own words how we have liberated you." The widow's accent unmistakably belonged to a Shoora. "Yes," Shoora said, "you liberated us; you liberated us from money, you liberated us from bread, and from sugar. To hell with your Stalin, the son of . . ." The station went off the air, but we knew where we stood. I was glad that I had not encouraged my sister to go to the east, from where the broadcast came. It was clear that the Soviet army had moved fast and that our brother Andrew's estate, where she had planned to stay, was by then some distance inside Soviet lines.

Tuesday, September 19, 1939

It seemed that every day started with efforts at protective measures. This day we were busy placing sandbags in the first-floor windows, especially those of the operating theatre.

An auxiliary ammunition dump in Saska Garden caught fire. Fortunately for us, it was a storage place for rifle bullets, rather than artillery shells. All day the cartridges exploded. It sounded as if big hailstones were falling on a tin roof.

By that time nothing should have surprised us. But the sight I witnessed that morning was not only surprising but entertaining. Zwerdling, with his red muffler and helmet, walked into the hospital, carrying on his back Countess Szoldrski, her hair ruffled, her eyes starting out of her head with terror. She was wearing Zwerdling's plush coat, and her bare feet showing.

Zwerdling carried her in, placed her on the table in the hall, and then tried to take back his coat. The countess protested, because she had nothing on under it but a nightgown.

Zwerdling, making a low bow, said, "Countess, I have seen all the colors of the rainbow," and with this remark he made off with his coat.

After attending to her wound, I tried to find out what had happened. I learned that the Countess had been working with Girl Guides when she was wounded. She was taken to the nearest hospital, which was accepting only wounded soldiers. Since that hospital could not admit her, one of the staff asked her whether she knew of any hospital that could. She had heard of Maltanski Hospital, and as her father was a Knight of Honor and Devotion in the Order of Malta, she asked to be sent to us. When the request came to us to pick her up, Zwerdling was sent to bring her, but we forgot to give him written authority. It is true that at first glance Zwerdling did not inspire confidence. Therefore, when the nurse on the ward saw him she refused to hand the countess over to him. But Zwerdling was resourceful, and when the nurse turned her back, he had kidnapped the patient in her hospital night-gown and slippers. (Later, on the way to Maltanski, she had lost the slippers.)

By now the question of blood transfusions had become more complicated. Though we had no means of typing blood, so many of the wounded were in dire need of immediate transfusion that we had to take chances. Originally we had had a register of volunteer blood donors, but when we sent for one it often happened that his house had been burned, or for some other reason he could not be found. One of our drivers, Jacek Goldman—the one who had found us an operating table—knew the location of many shelters, and he never failed to find someone who was willing to donate blood. That does not mean that he found such a person easily. Each time he had to tour a number of places. Goldman was on twenty-four-hour call.

All our staff had the same appearance—sunken cheeks, scorched lips, and black-rimmed eyes glittering from hunger and fever—but all had the same expression of determination. Not long before, each one had lived his own life, not knowing of the others' existence. One cause had gathered us together, and now, without any hesitation, each risked his own life if a fellow worker was in danger. When we worked on a rescue team, we acted in harmony, like an orchestra.

Food was on our minds. We often talked of it at night in the office-dormitory. We learned that close to the nearby racecourse was a field of cabbages and potatoes. It had not taken long—less than three weeks—to change our ethical values. The vegetable fields did not belong to us, yet we discussed whether we could raid them safely. We knew that the Germans were already on the racecourse, and we wondered whether the risk was too severe. The commandant said he would try to get these vegetables for us. The truck had been repaired; it could move. Of course all the messenger boys wanted to go, especially when they saw the commandant taking a shovel. We decided, however, to take three seminarians, who were strong and could work fast. Out they all went to the field.

Later, it was an exciting moment when the old, puffing truck, filled with cabbages and potatoes, stopped at our front entrance.

Apparently our team had not had an easy time. The Germans were entrenched on the racecourse, and when they saw people in the field they had fired artillery shells. The work had continued in spite of the shells, until the truck could hold no more. Then the group had had a terrible moment when the truck refused to budge. Fortunately, they had stopped the truck on a hillock, and by pushing they finally got the engine started, and were on their way. It was not the end; along the road they were shot at by machine-guns. The poor truck did its best. Making a superb effort, it reached ten miles an hour!

A truckload of potatoes and cabbages seemed impressive, but in reality it did not go very far; it amounted to one potato per person for the evening meal, and cabbage in the soup next day. But it did much for the morale of all.

Late at night we heard the rattle of carts. We went out, thinking it might be a big transport of wounded, but it was a group of artillery ammunition carts. The men in charge had lost their way, and so our commandant went with them to direct them to their destination. Less than fifteen minutes later, more such carts appeared; this time Roman went with them. Shortly afterward came yet another group. It seemed as if all the ammunition carts we had in Warsaw that night stopped at our door. It was then up to me to go with them, so I did. The night was bright with the moon and the light from burning houses. On my way back alone, a fifth column-ist shot at me from very close range. He must have been no further than ten feet away. I returned his shot, and took to my heels at a speed that could have won a quarter-mile race.

Wednesday, September 20, 1939

Every morning while I was visiting the wards, pieces of shells were swept out. Later that morning, I noticed in the hospital diary that sixteen pieces had been cleared from ward number three that day. Did it mean that the planks we had nailed up the day before were gone again?

All those shells bursting around but never inside the hos-pital made us feel that the hospital was shielded. Perhaps it was our prayers were helping; perhaps we were being saved for other tasks.

Monsignor Dobiecki performed his duties with dedication, as did his assistant and a few military chaplains who had come to us as patients.

One of those chaplains had been brought in the week before, wounded in the neck, not seriously, but painfully. He had been in bed only three days when he got up and trudged away to the vestibule of the bank in which we had installed the operating theater. There he sat in an easy-chair, solacing crowds of people waiting their turn for medical treatment or surgery. Miserable, suffering people, they lay on stretchers or even on the floor. Often the chaplain gave up his easy-chair and sat on the stone stairs, leaning his aching head against the wall. From early morning, when the first wounded were brought in, till very late at night, amid pools of blood and the moans of the suffering, the valiant man remained at his post.

The faith of the representatives of the church, the caliber of the chaplains in our hospital, and the work of Father Ostrowski in the city streets compensated for our great disappointment at receiving no word of sympathy from Rome when our country had been invaded. We felt abandoned by the Vatican at the time when we were giving our lives for the highest Christian values.

A fourteen-year-old messenger boy, Joseph, sent on an errand to the suburbs, unexpectedly met a German tank, which had broken through the barricades. He leaned his bicycle against a wall and, with a homemade bomb that someone handed to him, blew up the tank. Some say that when one is very near a tank, there is no danger. Joseph might have had such a notion, because he did not think it was anything outstanding to do. When he returned to the hospital, he hid himself. Why? Because that morning he had broken a bottle of red ink and was afraid he would be punished.

At noon someone left a parcel for me. With much curiosity I opened it and found my own coat, a box of chocolates, and a card telling me that the coat had been taken from my apartment as proof that the sender had been there. The note informed me that the sender had gone to my home to pilfer. While there he realized whose apartment it was. Since it was I who had administered first aid to his fellow worker and had dragged him into a protective gateway, he said he would steal nothing, and begged me to accept the chocolates in his name and that of his friend.

I was tempted to dip into the box right away. However, I thought that I needed some discipline and contributed it to Mrs. Deszert's store of candies.

In the executive council's office a few beds were set up at night, so we could rest. At first Stas and Roman rested there, later Dominik, then Josette, because her home was so far away from Maltanski. When the home of Senator Szymanski, our chief physician, was destroyed, he moved in. And recently the group had been joined by Mrs. Glinski, whose home in the suburbs was behind enemy lines, and by me, when I fled from my broom-closet "room" under the staircase after meeting a mouse face to face.

That night, in our office-dormitory, we discussed the incident of the near-thief who had returned my coat. We asked, what difference was there between a man who was called a thief and ourselves? We, the day before, had either participated in, or benefited from, raiding vegetable fields that did not belong to us. We had felt that hunger justified our deed; in fact we had been proud of it. Where should we draw the line? Under what circumstances could we take things belonging to someone else?

Before evening came waves and waves of bombers; the noise of explosions was like endless thunder. The bombing was concentrated on the "Old City"; the Cathedral and the Royal Castle were damaged again.

The Germans evidently realized that our allies would not create a second front, and that they could employ all their strength to crush our resistance. The advance of the Soviet Army seemingly had intensified the frenzy of their attack.

At the entrance to the hospital were crowds of wounded, to whom we all gave first aid. Those who could walk then had to go home because of the shortage of space. Sixty seriously wounded men, however, needed surgery. Both tables were used at the same time, also two chairs. Six surgeons, two of them over seventy, had been busy since early morning without respite. Each man's slice of bread had been brought to him in the operating theater.

Surgery always began immediately after the first air raid started, usually about seven A.M. Wounds from bombs were the most serious; they became infected within a few hours.

The news spread that the Army of Poznan, which had come to try to rescue us, was fighting close to Warsaw. That night there was a fierce battle.

Every evening at eight o'clock all the hospitals were required to sent headquarters a report as to how many wounded they had and how many more they could take. At nine o'clock each hospital received from headquarters a list of all the hospitals, with a statement of available accommodations, so that if we had no room, we would know where to send transports of wounded. That night all the hospitals were full except two, one of which could accept twenty patients and the other, thirty. But we knew that the fifty places might not be for more than an hour, with the increase in bombardment.

That night was a tragic one. The noise of the battle fought

by the Army of Poznan to break through to Warsaw sounded as though it were coming from the next block. The sky was flaming red. How many of our Polish boys would lose their lives trying to save the capital? For many of us the Army of Poznan was not just a name; it was our flesh and blood. Many of my close friends were serving with this army as reserve officers; my brother-in-law was a second lieutenant.

Maltanski was already overcrowded, and we had been ordered by headquarters to take no more wounded. At eleven o'clock several wagons and horse carts stopped at the entrance. The leader came in to report a tranport of eighty-two wounded from the Army of Poznan.

Doctor Fenski was in charge of the hospital that night. He used to be a civil-service physician, working on a health insurance program. Rules and orders were law for him. He was not too happy with our having to make changes constantly. Without an immovable structure it was difficult for him to function. He was shocked at the very idea of questioning an order or arguing against an official decision. He was in a dilemma and looked at me for help. I gave him the facts: At eight o'clock there were fifty hospital places available. We had orders not to take any more wounded, but here were eighty-two men on our doorstep.

It was an unforgettable moment, for I witnessed the rebirth of a man. The servile, frightened husks peeled off. The transformation was instantaneous. Here stood a man assuming responsibility for a decision contrary to orders but appropriate in terms of human compassion.

Dr. Fenski seemed to have grown physically. "If they have to lie on the floor elsewhere," he said, "we can find such a place here. Bring the wounded in."

There was no need to give special orders to arouse our staff from their sleep. All were at their posts in readiness. Mrs. Darska, who was in charge of the linen storeroom, had been dozing in an armchair in the hall, so that she would be on the spot to supply immediately whatever was needed. This woman was not young, and she had a bad heart condition.

Mrs. Darska began to work at once, bringing everything necessary for the wounded, and I went around the hospital with Mrs. Glinski in search of space.

In one ward while we conferred with the nurse, Aline, one of the nurses' aides, got up from the floor where she had been sleeping. She was a housemaid from Poznan, who had brought with her all she could save from her home—a pillow and a rug. "Here is my place, my pillow, and my rug," she said. "I can sleep very well without them, and we can take one boy more." That was but a single example among many of the readiness with which one and all willingly sacrificed their personal comfort and possessions for others.

When we returned to the hall the kitchen staff was already distributing hot tea.

Wounded soldiers were sitting or lying on the floor. We could not bother with formalities—registrations, identifications, and so on. Nurses came and, one by one, took whatever patients they felt they could tend in their wards. Surgeons were seeing which of the wounded needed surgery. Among the wounded was a man in civilian clothing whose shoulder was so badly dislocated that both bones were visible, about six inches apart. It was decided he would be attended to last, as his life was not in danger.

I was called to the operating theater, where the doctor showed me a sergeant badly wounded in the lung. When the wound had been dressed, and they were giving him clean linen, they noticed a wound in his hip that was so deep that the bone was visible. When the physician asked him why he had not mentioned it, he answered that he had had it for ten days, but that it was such a trifle that he thought it was not worth-while reporting. The sergeant was so anxious about his companion, already in the operating theater, that he refused to be wheeled to the ward until he was told his companion was expected to live. When we inquired, we learned that when the sergeant himself had been wounded the German armored vehicles were advancing. His companion, to cover the withdrawal of our troops, had set up a machine-gun in the middle of the roads while the tanks came closer and closer. He kept on shooting until he had stopped the first and biggest tank sixty yards in front of his machine-gun! After surgery, the doctor said this gallant lad would be saved. We placed him in the same ward as the sergeant.

By 3 A.M., all the men had been attended to but the one with the dislocated shoulder. His endurance impressed everyone, because, although his shoulder looked as though it must be hurting terribly, he still walked about and smoked cigarettes until his turn came. The doctors came around, some to help, some to look on. Though we were short of ether, we gave him as much as was considered necessary to set his shoulder. But all efforts to set the bones were unavailing; they would not move. In the middle of the pulling the man sat up, red with anger and pain. "When did it happen to you?" asked the surgeon. "In 1932," the man answered. He could not understand why we laughed so much.

Some may be curious, as we were, to learn where this man had come from. He had driven the truck that had brought the wounded to us. Since he understood that all treatment was free, a happy idea came into his head. Why should he not take advantage of this golden chance?

For the doctors the work was not yet over. After finishing here, they left to go to help at another hospital. It was the third night that they had done this. They would return at five or six, and an hour later would already be on duty in our operating theater.

Thursday, September 21, 1939

In the morning leaflets were dropped again:

POLES!
The German army has reached the line, Bialystok-Brzesc-Wlodzimierz-Stryj.

The towns, so-called, as well as the Polish fortifications, are occupied by the German Army.

Gdynia is captured. WARSAW, completely surrounded, must surrender immediately.

THE POLISH NAVY IS COMPLETELY DESTROYED.

THE POLISH ARMY IS TOTALLY DEFEATED.

The Polish detachments, surrounded near Kutno, are prisoners.

THE POLISH GOVERNMENT AND MARSHAL SMIGLY-RYDZ RAN AWAY TO ROMANIA.

THE RUSSIAN ARMY
on 9-17-39 at six A.M., crossed the East Polish frontier on the whole line and ATTACKED POLAND. Your leaders promised you that England and France would attack the Germans. And what are your so-called allies doing for you? Nothing and nothing! Your Polish Government therefore deceived you. Your allies deceived you.

POLES!
You fight without hope, and aimlessly. Why die? The Germans TREAT THEIR PRISONERS WELL AND CHIVALROUSLY. Your wives and children are waiting for you. Soon you will be able to work again for your families.

That is why: LAY DOWN ARMS! LONG LIVE PEACE!

We realized by now that there was no hope for us, that nobody was coming to our rescue. Still, we felt we had to continue to fight for what we believed, even if it would mean even greater sacrifices. We received leaflets like those, in brokn Polish, every day, and laughed at the spelling mistakes. We were angered by the claims that our leaders had run away, and we did not believe in the German "chivalry," as our experience provided evidence to the contrary. Nevertheless such leaflets did something to us subconsciously. We felt harassed and abandoned.

Rumors flourished. We believed in whatever would lift our morale. In our imaginations a western front weas a reality. We believed that Canada, Australia, and South Africa were preparing to send aid to the front, and that Berlin had been bombed several times. We believed that the British Army had landed in Gdynia, and we expected it in Warsaw any day.

Establishment of martial law was announced that day, with the death penalty for anyone who stole, tried to steal, or instigated theft. When posters announcing this appeared on walls throughout the city, we felt surprised that it had not been necessary until then to have martial law. All the stores and houses were open, for the doors and windows had been blown out. I wondered what value the commodities that ordinarily make life easier could have at a time when one might not live beyond the next few seconds.

An unexpected silence had followed the previous night's shelling. It was the result of an armistice—to last until four o'clock in the afternoon—to enable citizens of neutral countries to leave Warsaw. The streets were at once filled with people. Children played on the pavements, picking up "treasures"—splinters of bombs and shells.

The sun shone, and it was warm. How little one really needs to be happy!

I advised our staff to take a few hours rest, for their strength would be needed after four P.M. Everyone was to rest as much as was necessary during those eight hours of armistice, and devote the remaining time to preparing for return to his post.

I went to my own apartment and to my delight found that the bathtub and all the containers that I had filled with water at the beginning of the siege, according to government regulations, still contained water. There was no way to heat the water, but it was ecstasy to take a bath and change into clean linen.

On my way back to the hospital I met a few "pre-siege" acquaintances. To take advantage of the armistice they had left their shelters and were getting some fresh air. They had stayed in the deep basements of Staszic Archives, a safe place indeed. They told me about their experiences, and concluded, "You have no idea what we went through." It made me laugh at first, as I went on my way. I felt it was impudent for people who had not exposed a square inch of their skins to danger, who had just been waiting for things to be over, to tell me that I had no idea what they had gone through. Then I began to think they were right. To sit in darkness, hour after hour, day after day, doing nothing, must be terrifying indeed.

Also, I felt that remaining neutral, minding only one's own business, amounted to becoming, in a way, an accomplice of the enemy. Perhaps our hopeless fight in Warsaw, an open city with the only defenses those we erected in a few hours from buses, streetcars, and rubbish, had a purpose—a value for mankind. We were the first ones to say "No" to Nazism and to stand up for what we believed. So we stood behind those pitiful defense lines, with obsolete arms, a few planes soon shot down, a few anti-aircraft machine guns, a couple of artillery batteries, some rifles, a handful of soldiers, and unarmed civilian men, women, and children. We had stood for fifteen days against all the might of Germany in the first aggression in which it had met opposition.

In the first week of the attack Germany had announced the surrender of Warsaw, but then had to admit that the city was still fighting. It was more than a matter of their prestige to crush such resistance. The Nazi army had been indoctrinated for years to believe that their force was indomitable. To be stopped by a defenseless city could affect future moves.

I shivered at the thought of what it would be like after the neutral eyewitnesses had left and the armistice came to an end. No, I did not envy those in the safety of shelters. Right now I was not gripped by fear. This made me feel good.

When I had almost reached the hospital, I came upon a scene that moved me deeply. A big wagon, filled to overflowing with hospital bedlinen, was wobbling along with difficulty, pulled by a miserably skinny little horse, led by an old nun. A young nun was pushing the wagon from behind and steadying it whenever a wheel bounced over debris or a hole in the pavement so the cargo would not fall off. I asked them to wait, and said I would send a few men to help them in their task.

The problem of bedlinen was very serious. We had received tons of it in the first days, when gifts were flowing in. So much was needed when so much blood was being shed. Soiled things were thrown into the yard of a house that had been destroyed and was unfit for any other use. There they piled up.

At the onset of the siege we had made an agreement with a convent that the nuns would take responsibility for collecting the soiled articles directly from the place where we threw them, and launder them when they could. How these good nuns managed to wash the soiled articles without coal or soap was a mystery. The nuns with the wagon were apologetic; they said that they had managed to collect as much as each nun could drag at a time. But it was only that day that they had gotten hold of this horse, and they were happy to deliver a part of what they had laundered.

We were only too glad to take the collection and delivery out of their hands for that day, and did so without delay, taking advantage of the few hours of peace. We learned that they did the washing by hand in cold water from a well in their garden. They seemed unaware of the tremendous value of their service.

In those hours of the armistice, we had many social calls. Father Ostrowski visited us. At the beginning of the siege he had started a "mission center" in his family home, which we had previously inspected to see if it would be suitable for a hospital. He had gathered together priests, and day and night they went around the city, especially the most badly shelled areas. They gave absolution to the dying in the streets and encouraged and comforted people. They helped to take the wounded to the hospitals and rescued people and their belongings from burning houses. And they answered odd needs as they came across them.

We struck a bargain. Father Ostrowski had a few barrels of salted herrings, and we had horse meat. We knew that our wounded would have a great treat that night when they were given some herring, and the fathers would no doubt be glad to have a piece of horse meat. Both sides were pleased with the transaction.

Zwerdling was smart. While he was waiting in a car for the commandant in front of the Red Cross building, an officer had approached, drawn a revolver, got into the car, and told him to drive out of the city. According to the terms of the armistice, the barricades had been opened at a few points to let foreigners out. Zwerdling started without protest, but when he drove through the square where headquarters was located, he suddenly entered a place where he knew cars were not allowed. The military police stopped the car, and Zwerdling told them he was acting at a point of a gun. The officer was arrested. It turned out that he was one of the "Polish" officers who had entered Warsaw from German parachutes.

Soon after four P.M. the fight began anew.
The hall of the hospital, so shining and clean in the after-

noon, was again filled with wounded awaiting their turn in the operating theater. Those who were beyond assistance received an injection of the morphine which had been brought in that afternoon during the armistice by Dominik, who could get supplies from places no one else thought of. The medical staff welcomed this windfall, as such supplies were dangerously low.

In the daytime, whenever headquarters requested my services, I performed various emergency tasks. The nights were left to my discretion, and I spent them in my own headquarters, Maltanski. When it was possible every now and then, I got twenty minutes' sleep, which I felt was sufficient to let me function adequately.

That night I felt it was necessary to support the staff of our new civilian hospital in the bank building, half a block away. The patients came from the congested area of the city, which was inhabited mainly by Jews. They were screaming and moaning, especially those in the women's ward. Some of the moaning was due not to physical pain, but to other distress. In Poland, orthodox Jewish women have their heads shaved upon marriage, and then wear wigs. In the hospital, before the head was operated on, the hair had to be shaved off. Women not married, when recovering from the anesthetic, were in great distress when they realized that their heads had been shaved. The wailing in the women's ward was very trying to the nurses, so I spent much time helping them quiet patients and alleviate their distress.

The children's ward was the only silent one. They could not understand what had happened, why they suffered, why they had lacerated hands and legs. They were terrified and dared not even to whisper. One little girl was petting a doll she had made out of a small pillow. She herself had a torn foot, and was badly cut with glass. When I came to her bed, she whispered to me, "I tell my dolly that if she is good and does not cry, and is not afraid, when we go home I will give her a real big white roll." The other child in this bed seemed to me too quiet. I touched her—she was dead. The first child, consoling her doll, did not notice when the very small, thin body of an unknown girl was lifted out of her bed.

Carrying the little body through the hall, I heard a terrible, ghostly laugh. The hall was very large, dark, and empty. I wanted to drop the body and fly. Very quickly I carried the body and returned with a flashlight. On a stretcher in the corner of the hall lay an old woman in a pool of blood, laughing. It was weird. I sought out the doctor on duty to ask why the woman was lying there and had not been taken to the ward. I learned that her intestines had been torn out and that she was beyond assistance, so the doctor had given her an injection of morphine and left her in the hall, thinking she would die painlessly. But she had not died. She had gone mad from shock and pain. Contrary to all expectations, she lived for three days, singing about bread and coffee, only interrupting the song to laugh. That night I heard her again and again, all night long.

At midnight a shell burst on the top floor. The floor was empty, but I went to make sure that no fire had started. As I went up the staircase in the dark, that laugh followed me.

The civilian hospital—the bank—was a big building, and it took me some time to find the place where the shell had burst. There was no fire, but there was a hole in the wall through which I could see the city in flames. It looked like an ocean of fire, and it seemed as if not a single house would be left. The artillery shells were whistling as they passed the bank building.

An hour later a shell smashed a staircase, and another burst on the top floor. This time I asked a sentry to come with me, telling him that I did not know how to find the back staircase. The true reason was that I was afraid to go alone. Fortunately, no fire had broken out.

The children's ward remained silent. But every now and then a child would whisper to me that he wanted to say something, and when I would bend over, would grab my neck with frenzy, and pretending to have something important to communicate, would press his cheek against mine for comfort and protection. Many times I went around that ward "listening to secrets."

Two more shells struck the building, but did not explode. One hit the roof; the other, a particularly heavy one, pierced the wall on the top floor, and obstructed a passage-way. In the darkness one could easily stumble over it. It took the combined forces of Corporal Uptas and me to push it out of the way with our hands. I had a silly feeling performing tasks of this kind, something we had to do daily. Although rationally one knew that if the shell exploded there would not be much left of us, in the course of the work only our hands felt nervous. I felt that they were made of air; that they did not belong to the rest of my body.

I liked it when Corporal Uptas, who was in charge of the guards and sentries, was helping me. He felt strongly and on every occasion declared that nothing could be done successfully without his cooperation.

After the night in the civilian hospital I felt in need of some rest, and went to Maltanski. It was about five A.M. when I reached our office-dormitory. At that time the shelling was not so heavy in our area. Josette was sleeping like a baby. Under her bed two messenger boys had squeezed themselves for safety; other messengers were sleeping under other beds. Dominik, who slept from about midnight to six A.M., had his pajamas on over his uniform. My brother Stas was not there at the time; he was able to fall asleep for a few minutes and then to wake up whenever he wished. That night Roman had decided that it was not worth-while for him to try to sleep, because the wounded were trickling in one by one; each time he tried to rest he was called to collect arms. (I was no longer performing that task.) We had a glass of wine and a cigarette and we talked.

Roman was worried about being so afraid. I knew that though he never hesitated when he had to expose himself to great risk, his face would turn white. He knew it, and he said that everyone could see that he was afraid. He wondered what Stas and Dominik had that made them seem unconcerned when bombs were falling around them, or shells whistling. He asked what I did to not be afraid. Perhaps it was the wine, perhaps the tension of that night's experience, perhaps it was because his idea struck me as being so contrary to the truth, but I could not help laughing. I admitted that I was so saturated with fear that I could not be more afraid, and that he was wrong in thinking I was not afraid. I told him that in the civilian hospital, going upstairs in the dark to the accompaniment of the madwoman's laughter, I had felt that all the fear of the world was in me, I had accepted myself as being cowardly and had not pretended to be a heroine. I had taken off my mask of warriors and carried out my responsibility as well as I could. We had another cigarette and another glass of wine, and then I took a short nap before the next day would begin with whatever it should bring.

Friday, September 22, 1939

The previous night a sixteen-year old boy on our staff had gone out of his mind. At that age, when one is full of thoughts for the future, it is unbearable to see everything crashing, destroyed—blood everywhere—so many dead bodies that it is difficult to find room to bury them.

An ambulance had been carrying wounded to us nearly every day. I did not know where it belonged, but it did not matter. Another boy of sixteen used to accompany the ambulance, and he was always anxious to know if there was room for "his wounded." That boy had something striking about him, something one could not forget. He had enormous black eyes, which always began to shine when he was told that we would make room for "his wounded." He carried a red squirrel in his pocket; she would pop her head out and look around curiously. That morning when the ambulance brought casualties, there was another boy with them. When I asked the driver the reason for this change, he said, "We went to the front lines last night. He went to pick up soldiers, and he . . . he will not come any more."

Several shells burst simultaneously in our garden, and we heard the noise of broken trees and branches. "O heaven! the cows must have been killed!" I went out to see, and they were alive. Trembling, they pressed toward me. They also must have felt for a short while the need for a human being. But I had no time for them. There had been enough sorrow already that day, and I did not know what would still come. I satisfied myself that the cows were alive, gave them a little pat, and was off.

That day the Hospital of the Child Jesu was bombed, and many of the wounded were killed. Those bombings of hospitals were not accidental. We had little doubt that hospitals were special targets.

Shortly after the Germans attacked us, the hospitals had removed the Red Cross emblems from vehicles carrying wounded, for if the Red Cross signs were clearly discernible on a vehicle, a plane would dive to machine-gun it. Such vehicles kept their flags inside, waving them only to get priority and help from the citizens when the road was blocked.

The Hospital of the Child Jesu was so big that it could not be missed. When its walls began to fall, the staff took the surviving patients to stretchers on the lawn, thinking they would be safer there, where no wall could fall on them. A

German pilot, however, dived and shot the wounded soldiers
with his machine gun, giving them the lethal blow. Among the
personnel there were also many casualties.

The water supply failed. Could it be restored that time?
Dominik went to the city hall to inquire.

A young nurse carrying a cup of hot milk was going to
the corridor, with tears running down her cheeks. "What is
the matter?"

"This milk is so hot and smells so delicious. It is for the
patient who had his arms amputated last night, and I am so
terribly hungry."

A report came from Mrs. Tarnowska, head nurse in our
second military hospital: It had been shelled. Its walls were
outlined against the sky; and all the doors had been blown in.
At any moment the building might fall. The wounded had to
be evacuated. But to where? It was late at night, and though
very tired, I went to the place. Upon arriving, I stopped at
the door for a short rest. Nobody saw me. The wounded soldiers were huddled together on the floor of the hall, in the
guttering candle light.

One of them, the sergeant, was sitting on the corner of a
table, calmly speaking words of confidence and trust: "It is
nothing, boys, if they destroy us, burn us, kill us. Death comes
only once. And to lose a fortune, a hand, a leg, or life itself
for what one believes, for a holy cause—one has to do it. If
the whole of Poland be occupied—if it be completely destroyed
—we shall rise again; so don't worry boys. . . . Boys, if we get
out alive, we shall never forget these moments, or what everyone is doing for us."

I had thought the raid was over, but then a bomb fell with
a nerve-racking wail. (Occasionally some device was added
to a bomb to produce this effect.) It fell near the hospital,

close to that wall behind which the soldiers were sitting. There was a heavy thud. Then the stillness was deathlike; there was no explosion. The soldiers began to pray: "Who places himself under God's protection, and with his whole heart sincerely trusts Him. . . ."

I slipped away quietly—there was still much to do, and in my judgment there was no immediate danger.

Josette took charge of the evacuation. During the night she found some cellars in nearby houses, large enough to hold all the wounded, and at daybreak they were evacuated, three or four at a time. Even the furniture—beds, tables, and chairs —were moved.

Saturday, September 23, 1939

None of our staff could rest even during the early hours. The wounded were brought in a steady stream. The personnel were almost at the end of their resources. How long would it all last?

The Army of Poznan had been beaten. We felt ourselves more and more isolated.

The electric power station had been definitely destroyed. We had no light, and knew we would have none in the immediate future.

When the radio became silent, we were cut off from the world. That feeling was the worst of everything we had experienced.

That day the operating theater worked ceaselessly; delicate operations were performed by candlelight.

Mrs. Deszert came that morning to my office, all upset over a "dreadful" thing that had happened in Maltanski Hospital, of all places—moreover, almost next door to the chapel. She

had kept her treasure of sweets in the telephone booth, and
had only turned her back for a moment, when someone stole
a handful of candies. She would have to count them all to
establish exactly how many had been taken. Mrs. Deszert went
on lamenting, and I had to go to the scene of the crime to see
for myself. I felt that Mrs. Deszert did so much for the morale
of the hospital, that the least I could do was to give full attention to a problem that was important to her. Her main concern
was how she would account for the loss in her little green
book, which would become a part of the Malta archives. She
felt it would be shameful to have to record in black and white
that we had a thief on our staff. I said that we did not know
who it was—it might have been a fifth columnist.

Before leaving, I asked for a few candies for the messenger
boys. She gave me a number, for which I signed. In the hall
the boys were in readiness at their post. "Boys, there are
sweets for you!" Their eyes flashed with joy. The youngest,
Andrew, smiled; his lips were so scorched that they cracked
and bled.

One of our soldiers was really lucky. As he was being
carried out of the ward to have his dressing changed, a bomb
had burst in our garden. His bed, which was near the window,
was pierced by two splinters. Several of the wounded were
thrown out of bed, but no one was hurt.

At first we felt that the worst possible thing was that the
telephone did not work. Thanks to the messengers, however,
communication had not been entirely severed, so we had
suffered more emotionally than otherwise. It had not occurred
to us that we might later be without light and water.

That morning we had to consider what we should do about
light. The supply of candles was dwingling; even with great
economy they could last for only two or three days. Dominik
said he was certain that somewhere in Warsaw there must be

a supply of oil lamps or spirit lamps, and that he would go and search for them.

Dominik's home had been bombed the night before, and that had done something to him. Dominik was a connoisseur of antiques, and his home was an art object itself. It was his main love and interest in life. We felt that we should keep Dominik moving, for when one runs toward something one can at the same time run away from something else.

We were still on the problem of light when Monsignor Dobiecki came. War or no war, he said, one cannot condone pilfering because it is a small matter compared with the one we were just considering. Small matters, he said, bring a sense of proportion and keep our feet on the ground.

After this introductory sermon, he told the story of the "Lombroso" incident. This soldier, the reader will recall, had been court-martialed and was about to be executed for murder. He had been wounded when the prison in which he was being held had been bombed. Our hospital for him meant getting well for the sake of death by execution, so he had constantly kept tearing off his bandages, and finally died of gangrene.

Early in the morning, his family and former pals came to claim his body. How they knew he was in Maltanski or that he had died was baffling. While claiming the body, they stole a sheet. Monsignor got indignant, imposed a fine on the family, and had refused to release the body until the sheet was returned and the receipt from our office for the fine shown to him. "Lombroso" was out of our hands; let his soul at last rest in peace.

I asked the messenger boys to get me a doll when they had the opportunity. One of them was lucky enough to come upon a store where the owner was piling up his goods for protection, and when the boy stated our request he was given a beautiful doll. I took the doll to the Jewish children's ward, where she sat on a different bed every hour. The children looked at her but did not touch her. She belonged to a civilized world from which we were cut off. They preferred to play with dolls made out of pillows, which, being without legs and arms, were more like themselves.

We were alarmed about the commandant, who had gone with Dominik to search for lamps, but had not yet returned. His party told us that when grenades had begun to burst all around them, they had taken shelter in a gateway. When the smoke had cleared somewhat, he could not be found, and they had come back without him. Two hours later he returned. He said he had not wanted to waste time waiting in a shelter, and so had walked to the Red Cross. It was lucky he had done so, because he was given 650 ampules of various solutions for injections, which he carried back to Maltanski.

Whenever the commandant was overdue, I became very anxious. That was not the first time I had worried when he did not return when expected.

At first, an executive would go out alone with a driver. Later, however, when going out became increasingly dangerous, Dominik, who was the Malta delegate for Warsaw and thus the highest authority in our corps, decided that we should go in pairs, as it would be good for our morale. Partners were changed every few days. That day Dominik decided that from then on I would go with my brother, and he himself would go with Roman. It was a great relief for me.

Late in the afternoon chef Kwiecinski came to the office in great indignation, to tell us it was shocking that we had not yet had our breakfast. I felt that whether I had eaten, breakfast or not, was my personal concern. Perhaps the tone of his voice nettled me; perhaps the pang of hunger when food was mentioned added the critical straw to the stress of handling big and small matters all mixed together. Anyhow, my few polite words, thanking him for his consideration, but pointing out that my welfare was my personal matter, contained more venom than a hundred cobras could produce.

Chef Kwiecinski was hurt. He said that more was involved than the executives' welfare, for which he personally cared. He reminded me that because we were all volunteers risking our lives and working for the same cause, I should have more understanding of his effort. His staff was hungry; they received the same rations as the rest of us, and were handling food. He would have protected the piece of bread for my daily ration from anyone who might feel that since I did not care, it could be taken. This task would add to his burden, for once his staff started biting into rations that were not theirs, discipline would be gone. He stated that I did not understand the circumstances under which his department worked, and never gave a word of praise, taking everything for granted.

While this philippic was being delivered, I realized how right Kwiecinski was. I apologized for having hurt him, and remarked that often we take for granted something that does not happen automatically but is really due to some person's effort and efficiency. We felt lucky that due to his leadership our wounded were fed, I said, because it was not the case in several other hospitals. I told him that as soon as we had finished the matter at hand, we would come for breakfast.

When Chef Kwiecinski had left, triumphant, Dominik said that since I made such good use of Monsignor Dobiecki's sermon and since my feet were now well on the ground, we might go and have something to eat.

Behind the kitchen was a large pantry, with thick walls—it had been built in a pre-icebox area. It had a small window, almost as high as the ceiling. It was an ideal place for a meal, being sheltered from the bombing, if not from the noise. One would hardly know a war was on.

But it was meant in the design of our fates that we would not eat this breakfast. As soon as we were seated at a table, which was really a shelf, shrapnel burst just outside our quiet little place, and splinters hit the lamp, which shattered into a thousand pieces all over our bread and cocoa, and threw everything together on the floor. A nurse who was about to enter the kitchen fell to the ground, blood gushing from her neck. I knew that when blood spurts out in rhythm it comes from an artery. I therefore pressed her neck below the injury and stopped the bleeding, but she was losing consciousness, and I hoped competent help would arrive on time. It did, and when the nurse had been carried out, and the attending physician had reported that her injury was not fatal, we returned to the pantry.

During the shrapnel incident we had observed another of Chef Kwiecinski's attributes, his thunderous voice. When the shrapnel burst, his kitchen staff, mostly women, screamed and hid under the tables, but his voice brought them out and back to work.

Though there was no breakfast, Chef Kwiecinski brought us a bottle of champagne, which was much tastier and more effective than cocoa made with water.

Before evening something terrible began to take place in the sky. Dep yellow and black clouds whirled, and the noise in the sky was even louder than it was on the ground, where artillery fire and bombing were constantly going on. It seemed as if some infernal powers were waging a battle. None of us remembered having seen anything like it in our lives. Perhaps rain would fall. We hoped for rain and prayed for it. Lately there had been so much smoke that we could not see the sky. It seemed as if the smoke had cleared only for this display. Hailstones as big as chestnuts began to fall. The ground became white, and the weather bitterly cold. Heaps of hailstones still lay on the ground at noon next day.

We had had no ice for two weeks, and ice was so necessary in a hospital that I felt it might be a good idea to place pails and basins in the back yard to collect the hail. It proved to be a regrettable idea, for we had no sooner put them in the yard than shrapnel burst. No one was injured, but all the pails and basins became sieves. This was serious because there was no possibility to get new ones.

Night came. Would we live through it? There was no thought of sleep or rest for any of the staff. We organized rescue teams in case we should be struck. In the wards, without light, the wounded were very restless.

I went to see Mrs. Tarnowska to ask what her prospects were, now that our military hospital number two was housed in the cellars of several houses. She did not feel that she would need our help; she had reliable leadership in every segment of her hospital, which was well sheltered.

In the civilian hospital the danger was from fire, so we had a few sentries who checked each time the upper floors were hit, to see that a fire did not start.

Maltanski was the hospital in danger and in need of vigilance.

Late at night, going through the wards, I noticed a soldier whose face was buried in a pillow. He was sobbing and screaming into the pillow, so that he would disturb no one. The nurse told me that he had meningitis, and there was not much that we could do to relieve his pain. In his hopeless condition and agony, that boy had consideration for others. I looked at my hands and felt that I might be able to help him. If I could transmit vibrations in harmony through the piano, why could

I not transmit harmony directly, without an instrument?
When I took the boy's head in my hands, he grabbed them
with such force that I thought his nails would be imbedded
in my flesh. I prayed that the harmony of the world would
come to help me alleviate his pain. He stopped screaming, his
sobs quietened down, and then his hands released their grip
and he was asleep.

A sentry looked for me. He had noticed that every fifteen
minutes a number of shots were fired in the distance; then
they were heard near us, and then repeated, further in the
distance. He wondered what it was about, especially since
the shooting near us seemed as if it was coming almost from
our own yard.

I went out with the commandant and Roman. We soon
realized that the shots were sounding out messages in Morse
code. Fifth columnists seemed resourceful; when electricity
failed they substituted this simple device. Roman went at once
to report it to headquarters, and returned with an order for
us to catch the spies and deliver them to headquarters. It
proved to be no problem; eight sentries, with the commandant
and Roman, caught six while they were transmitting the
signals. To deliver them to headquarters was the problem,
and on the way two escaped. This link, however, was out of
order for the night. The fifth columnists would have to think
of something else.

Sunday, September 24, 1939

During the previous night a beautiful oak tree that grew in
front of Maltanski's porch had been ripped up by its roots.
Bombs sometimes do strange things. It seemed as if a gigantic
hand had picked the tree up and thrown it on its side.

As it was Sunday, some people prophesied that the day would be quieter; others, that the churches would be a special target. It turned out that none of them were right, for artillery shells as well as bombs bursted everywhere.

The streets were deserted. The Opera House had been burned. Senatorska Avenue, on which Maltanski Hospital was located, had scarcely a house that was not either levelled or gutted. That was how all the main streets looked. Driving, one had to keep to the main streets; the days when we could dodge into a side street to avoid machine guns were over, for those streets were blocked with rubble.

All our cars were damaged, some beyond repair. The good old truck, the last of the Mohicans, which had an improvised garage in a gateway, was found that morning as a heap of scrap.

Dominik solemnly declared when we met that morning that he would find lamps for our operating theater and all the others in Warsaw if it was the last thing he did.

Incendiary bombs fell, setting fires near the hospital; and, as there was no water, it was impossible to fight them. We watched the fires with concern because if they came a little nearer, they would directly threaten us.

It is strange how in the midst of mass destruction some individual achievement seems important. That morning our rescue teams performed work in which several hundred people were saved. The staff received due recognition, and a report was sent to headquarters. But everyone here was rejoicing about Corporal Uptas's having saved a child. Perhaps the reason was that such events occur also in peacetime. A house had been in flames from top to bottom for nearly an hour, when a woman came running, screaming that her child was in a flat on the fourth floor. (She had gone to gossip with a friend around the corner.) Defying the flames, Corporal Uptas ran up, tied the child to his back with his belt, and slid down the banister through the fire. A few messenger boys stared in awe and admiration, and some people left their cellars to watch. Corporal Uptas handed the child over to his mother, and she kissed the corporal to the delight of all. Corporal Uptas spent every minute he could spare writing down the story for the hospital diary. He described the achievement of Corporal Uptas as if he were writing about someone else, praising his courage and daring, and then he duly signed the story and handed it to Miss Maciejewska and watched to make sure that she pasted it into the diary at once.

Dominik brought us fifty lamps for methylated spirits. We shall never know where he ferreted them out from. If we could get methylated spirits from somewhere the operating theaters would have light that night.

Dominik was mysterious; he told us that we should soon have a most exciting experience. The cars, he said, must be put in order; the drivers would have to do their best. We were to start in two hours.

Dominik loved adventures, and so did the commandant and I. Although we were tired, he managed to arouse our spirit of adventure. "You will have fun this time," he said, to make us more impatient. He was always smiling; it was not a mask. He was always extremely cool, and that coolness might on occasions have been a mask. (I think he was the only man in Warsaw, except the commandant, who shaved every day during the siege.)

At last, when the cars were ready, Dominik told us that we were to go across the Vistula to the district of Praga, to take all the methylated spirits we could from a Government depot, parts of which had been burning for twenty-four hours.

The fire could be seen from a distance as a clear blue light, waving and dancing as if drunk.

The storehouses we were going to stood on both sides of a street, and there was fire on both sides. That fire was unpredictable; it leaped across the street, and then held back and seemed to quiet. It was the most unusual conflagration I had ever seen. We had to reach the end of the street, which was blocked by a building that had collapsed. The storehouses not yet on fire were at the end of the street. Dominik seemed a little anxious; he said that in the morning the fire had not seemed so vast. We loaded the cars with 1000 gallons of methylated spirits in one-gallon and half-gallon cans. It was hazardous, for although the storehouse from which we were taking the cans was not yet burning, the neighboring one was. At last the cars were filled. The cans, however, were not airtight. The alcohol was evaporating; and we feared that a spark could cause an explosion.

By the time we were ready to leave, there was a curtain of fire across the street, how thick we did not know. Dominik laughed a little uneasily and said, "Afterward they will tell us it is impossible to go through fire with explosive material, and they will be talking nonsense!" His car was to leave first. It backed up as far as the debris permitted, to get up speed, then dashed forward, rushed onto the sidewalk to avoid the brunt of the fire, which was raging in the middle of the road, and disappeared in the midst of the flames. A short time later, though it did not seem at all short to us, we heard the sound of his horn—he was safely through.

Next came my turn. In the car, beside the driver, was Andrew, the messenger boy. It was his most dangerous expedition, and he was white. "Andrew," I said, "it will not be shameful at all if you do not go with us. You can slip through the other side of those destroyed houses and return to the hospital." Andrew looked at me with angry eyes. "Will you go with me?" he said. We took our places in the car. It was a big, heavily loaded Buick. Like Dominik, we backed up slowly, as far as possible. We gathered as much speed as we could, rushed onto the sidewalk, and were surrounded by flames. The cans inside made an infernal noise. Speed! Speed! The car jumped terribly; we hit something. Like lightning, the thought passed through my head; would it be the end? Not now and not here, please, God. The next moment we were in an open space, out of the fire. We stopped. I got out, and noticed that I was still repeating: "Speed! Speed!" Those 200 yards had seemed endless. We sounded the horn for the last car to start. Time was short, for the fire seemed to grow bigger every moment. The commandant was in the third car. It sprang out of the fire. Thank God, we were all safe!

On our way back to the hospital we noticed a big abandoned truck. Our thoughts by now were well synchronized, for each of us, although in different cars, had the same idea. "As soon as we get to the hospital and unload, we must go back and take that truck, to replace our ruined one." We went back, but in the meantime it had been bombed.

Father Ostrowski came before evening to say good-bye, for he was sure he would be killed that night. We talked for a short while; he was as gay as usual, and left to do his work of helping people in the streets.

In the evening Roman received a message that a son had been born to his wife. It was their first child. Superstition holds that the birth of a boy during a war foretells a long war, but Roman was happy nevertheless. He went to see his son, and returned about midnight, full of the beauty and cleverness of his child.

After midnight the maternity hospital where Roman's wife had given birth to their baby was bombed and caught fire. Roman's wife took her baby, walked out of the hospital, and spent the rest of the night crouched in a gateway. At daybreak she carried her baby home.

Monday, September 25, 1939

That day it was bitterly cold. The planks in the windows had been blown out again. We had a few planks to replace them, but no nails to fasten them. The wind blew freely through the wards. We felt helpless.

The well, which was at that time our only source of water, was nearly empty, and what water that was left was dirty.

The little mimeographed bulletin that we called a newspaper was not appearing any longer.

Though there was a feeling of being in the grave, our resistance was not broken.

From early morning hundreds of planes bombed us. It was the worst day we had had. The roaring was terrible—the roar of bursting bombs, the roar of crackling shells, and the roar of falling houses.

Another bomb imbedded itself in the roof of Maltanski. We were lucky that it did not explode.

A great many bombs and shells that had not exploded were lying around everywhere.

Rumor spread that Great Britain was landing an army at Danzig and Konigsberg to help us, and that the Soviet Union was at war with Germany. Everyone, whether wounded or staff, began to wonder how long it would take the British motorized units to get to Warsaw. We were certain that we were now in the last days of our torture. We thought that the present fury of the attack was the vengeance of the Germans before their withdrawal from Warsaw, which would take place if Great Britain, with all her power, sent help to Poland. Meanwhile the bombing continued.

Anyone with the slightest notion of geography would know that such help was not possible as long as Germany had a navy

and an army, but the need to feel that someone cared was as
strong collectively as individually. Perhaps in the back of his
head one knew it was not quite so, but the necessity for cling-
ing to hope was great; and we clung to it.

Three incendiary bombs fell on the roof of our storehouses;
thank God, the sentry saw them and put the fire out.

The kitchen was slightly damaged during the night, but in
spite of the damage we were served a very excellent "neighing
soup."

We decided to bury the cans of ether that were not immediately needed, and part of the methylated spirits that we
had brought the day before, the part we felt we should keep
for our own use. It was important to remove explosive material from the hospital. We would take the bulk of the
methylated spirits and most of the lamps to other hospitals
for their operating theaters.

I went to look for Roman, as it was our task to bury our
share of the cans of ether and to plan the distribution to other
hospitals. In the bank that we used as an annex, we had
arranged a dormitory where the men could take short naps
when opportunity permitted. I found Roman there. We took
shelter in the doorway, with shells bursting around us. Roman
told me that he had learned that his wife had reached home
safely, but that he was worried about her health, since she
had had to walk a distance a few hours after confinement.
Roman was thirty and his wife twenty-four. He hoped that
in the evening he might have some time free to visit her.
Roman was holding a glass of water in his hand. "You see,"
he said, "I procured a glass of water and hoped to shave myself in honor of my son, but I will do it later on. It is cold
water, so it can wait."

When he had brought the cargo of spirits to Maltanski, we
deposited it in the entrance of an empty building in the neigh-

borhood. While we were working, a shell burst in an upper story, and the building began to burn. We worked in great haste. Some of the cans were leaking and we wanted to avoid an explosion. Everyone in the vicinity helped. Leaving as much as we needed for that day, we buried the rest. The cargo for distribution was loaded in cars.

Then we had to go to the city to deliver the spirits and the lamps to various hospitals. I was so afraid that I felt faint. We had a short conference and traced the routes for Dominik and Roman and for the commandant and me. We were taking the big Buick, and planned to stop on the way back at a factory where medical supplies had been manufactured, to requisition some things we needed urgently.

Before leaving I remarked to Dominik that lives might be saved that night because he had obtained the lamps and the spirits so that the operating theaters in Warsaw would have light. I felt as if he were far away. His mask of warriors was down. This was not the carefree chief of staff, who was never afraid, but a human who could take no more. He said it might be, after all, the last thing he did; he could watch this butchery no longer; he did not wish to live in a world of violence. He had done what he could, but he was desperately tired and wanted to have a rest. Roman, who was already taking his place in the car and wanted to get this expedition over with, called to him. Dominik joined him and they were off.

I was shaken; it was not what he said, because Dominik's mask had never been airtight, and even in the past I could see how much compassion it concealed.

We delivered the lamps and the spirits to the hospitals. They were glad and surprised to receive such gifts. Dominik liked to do things that were considered impossible, things that no one else would think of. A few days earlier, we would have visited the hospital staffs and basked in their gratitude and admiration, for we were proud of the reputation of Maltanski

Hospital for being helpful, and we were proud of our rescue teams, which were courageous and efficient. That day, however, we wanted only to get rid of a dangerous cargo and return to Maltanski. To meet an emergency the hospital had only Mrs. Glinski, Josette, Monsignor Dobiecki and Senator Szymanski—half the usual strength.

We had one more journey to make—to the factory. That meant a long stretch on the main avenue. A plane hunted us with machine-gun fire all along the way; the pilot seemed determined to get us. He made passes from different directions. In our effort to escape we had to speed, avoiding bomb craters and all sorts of obstacles. For once the dense smoke was of some use; though we could not see even a few yards ahead, and we felt sure that the pilot could not see us either. Later we noticed that there were bullet holes in the back of the car. By that time, though, we had become indifferent to danger; it seemed merely a nuisance.

When we arrived at the factory we found it blazing. Chemicals were exploding, producing a cacophony like the tuning of an orchestra. It was disappointing to have to return empty-handed. As we passed my apartment house, I asked my companions, the commandant and Jacek Goldman, who was driving, to stop and let me get a case of champagne that I had bought for a party to celebrate my first world concert tour, which I had given up. I felt a need to have something real in the face of the make-believe expectation that the British Army was on the way from Danzig. We took the case quickly and drove back to the hospital.

We were astonished that Dominik and Roman had not come back, because their destination had been nearer than ours.

I could not get over a feeling of pain when I thought of Dominik. That morning he had seemed to have given up. Each time that I had noticed this sign of having given up, whether in a member of our staff, in a wounded soldier in the ward, or in anyone else, that person had died within a day.

We received an SOS from the city hospital, which was caring for thousands of wounded soldiers and civilians. The hospital had been shelled by artillery since daybreak, and was on fire. Since early morning it had been an inferno.

As for helping the victims of the fire, I had to consider whether we had the right to leave our own hospital, for when night approached, fear would increase and one could feel vibrations of anxiety rising in the whole hospital. We felt that we—the commandant and I—could not make the decision to take rescue teams and go without having the agreement of those who would have to be responsible for the safety of Maltanski.

We sent messengers to call the head nurses of the wards and the chiefs of services. These included Chef Kwiecinski, Corporal Uptas, the head storekeeper, and the head stretcher-bearer. We told them of the call for help, and asked whether they felt that they could take responsibility for their various services and be available where needs arose, knowing that they could not depend on our help. They accepted unanimously. And so the commandant headed one rescue team and I the other, and we went to the city hospital.

The situation there was desperate. The place looked like a furnace; every two minutes a heavy artillery shell burst. The aiming at the hospital was so precise that houses surrounding it were left untouched. This hospital was a huge place, with a great number of buildings. Some were on fire from top to bottom, just blazing masses; others had been hit but were not yet burning.

No hospital of that size would have sufficient stretchers to carry out such a huge number of wounded at the same time, nor the staff needed to assist in so gigantic an evacuation. Some of the wounded were fortunate enough to have been carried out; others were pulled down the stairs and dragged across the ground; some, though badly wounded, tried to crawl away to get out of reach of the flames.

The rescue operations were not co-ordinated, and under such circumstances they could not have been. I did not know where the commandant's team was working. With my team, I decided to work in a building from which we heard women's screams. The staircase was on fire, and there was not much time left for that floor; the fire was advancing. Some soldiers came running with a ladder. They placed it against a window and climbed in, but there was no time to carry patients individually down one ladder. The fire had reached the corridors. The rescuers began to throw the women out of the windows onto coats or whatever we held out for them.

I recognized one of the women, as a few days before I had picked her up from the streets, wounded. She had told me on the way that she was the wife of a policeman, and that she had been married just before the siege. Both of her legs had been torn off. For the second time I helped this agonized woman.

We worked as long as work could be done. Artillery fire grew increasingly heavier, concentrating on the blazing mass, where about 400 wounded soldiers and a number of civilians, and several nurses and doctors of the hospital staff and rescue teams had been burned alive.

After reaching our hospital late in the evening, we found that Dominik and Roman had not returned. We did not dare to speak about it, but every one of us had the same thought; if there was a spark of life left in them, they would let us know. We sent a message to Roman's wife, telling her that he could not come that night. Would he ever come?

Father Ostrowski was killed, not the night before as he had expected, but that morning at nine o'clock. He and his priests had been assembling for breakfast at the Ostrowski Palace when it was struck by a stick of bombs, killing them all. It was not possible to count the victims or to identify them. The work of helping people where they were, in streets or homes, came to an end.

A group of six doctors from the city hospital came to join us. They no longer had a hospital, and wondered whether we could use their services. Indeed we could. They were exhausted and still dazed after the day's experience in the city hospital. We gave them some wine and looked for a place where they could sleep for the night. One of them, a woman, lost her way in the darkness of the top floor, and, not knowing that one staircase had been destroyed, fell and broke her neck.

After midnight I became a bartender, as a glass of wine and a cigarette at this time seemed to be more helpful than anything else. Members of the staff would come, drink a glass, sit for a few minutes, say a few words or not say anything, and then return to their posts. Mrs. Glinski came at about three A.M. and suggested that we take some wine and a little bread to the operating theater. Chef Kwiecinski had kept a few slices for an emergency. In the operating theater an emergency indeed had arisen. Amputation of a leg was in progress. The nurse administering anesthetic was tottering. Mrs. Glinski stepped in and told her to sit down and take a slice of bread and a sip of wine. That, however, was not all. The surgeon, who was the old colonel—nearly eighty years of ago—stood dazed and unable to proceed with the operation, though the bone was ready to be sawed. It did not occur to him to ask a nurse to saw the bone; nor would any nurse take the initiative, even under such circumstances. There was no time to waste. I had no tradition in medicine whatsoever, and therefore it seemed natural to me to take the saw from his hand when he held it toward me. I asked a young nurse to serve him some bread and wine. In my street coat, with hands which had not been recently washed, I asked the nurses for directions on how to proceed with the amputation. They pointed to the exact place where the bone was to be sawed, and I sawed it. By that time the colonel had regained strength, and he finished the operation.

Behind the operating theater was the strong-room. There we sheltered the smallest children—the children of the staff, my sister's children, and some orphans, whom we had found wandering hungry, homeless, and distressed in the streets. The children could hear the groans from the operating theater, and were sickened by the smells of ether and blood.

Seeing me come in, a boy, perhaps two years old, began to scream: "No bombs; no bombs!" Poor little one! I had taken him out of a house when it was struck by a bomb, and later on from a cellar when that house caught fire. He was the only child in my whole experience of the siege who showed fear and screamed. The most heartbreaking thing was the matter-of-fact calm with which the children reacted to the harrowing experiences to which they were exposed.

Tuesday, September 26, 1939

Before daybreak the commandant and all the drivers went to search for Dominik and Roman. Josette was in my office; we had nothing to say.

At about six o'clock the commandant returned. Before he said a word, we already knew. He went to his desk, and placed on it a pair of broken spectacles that had belonged to Roman and watches, documents, and trifles. Then he said, "We looked for the car, and spotted it. They did not suffer; they were killed outright by shrapnel. It burst in front of the car and wounded them both in the forehead. It happened on their way back. Dominik had promised that the hospitals in Warsaw would have light in their operating theaters, and had kept his word. The operating theaters did their work last night, as did

ours, with lamps instead of candles. We must ask the chaplain
to bury them; they still lie on the sidewalk."

We went to the bank where the men had a room to rest in
—the commandant, Josette, and I. On the window sill I saw
Roman's glass of shaving-water. It did not take us more than
a few minutes to pack their things.

We had to resume our duties. The day had begun with a
still heavier bombardment than that of the day before. The
hospital seemed empty without those two men. How much
they had meant to it! They were buried before noon in a
common grave, dug in a flower bed in the street. Monsignor
Dobiecki blessed their graves. None of us could attend, for
the situation in Maltanski was serious, and we could not leave
our work.

That day we had no bread. The wounded, shivering with
cold, were hungry. Our cows were a blessing; they mooed
with fear, but they gave milk, which was given to the children
and to a few wounded whose lives depended on having something to eat. For the past few days the Red Cross had delivered
bread. That day we wondered whether they had it, but could
not deliver it. The commandant went with me to find out. If
we could have a slice for each of the wounded it would mean
much for their morale. Josette took charge of the hospital.

Driving was an excruciating experience. The smoke, however, protected us a little from the watchful eyes of German
pilots and their machine guns. We found the Red Cross building in ruins. We drove to the other party of the city to Red
Cross headquarters; it was in flames and abandoned.

It is strange what things attract one's attention in a situation
like the one we were in at that moment, with planes overhead
bombing us and chasing us with machine-gun fire, and artillery
shells bursting all around. If I had to tell what stood out in my
memory that morning when driving around the city, I would
name two incidents. A bomb struck a house in front of us,

and out of the third-floor window came clouds of feathers.
Further on our way, another bomb struck a five-story house;
the whole front became detached and tottered precariously.
We speeded to pass before it blocked the street; then it crumbled. We were glad to have been able to pass; otherwise we
would have had to abandon the car, which was our last one.

It was almost noon. Stas was determined to look further for
bread, but we felt that one of us should return to the hospital.
It was not far away, and I could reach it quickly on foot,
taking short cuts. On the way I passed my apartment house.
The roof was on fire, and out of my glassless windows the
drapes were waving.

Our artillery had ceased firing. The enemy planes flew just
above the housetops. The wounded were brought from the
front lines, from the streets, and from other hospitals, until
Maltanski was so full that it was difficult to walk through it
without stumbling over someone.

In the previous twenty-four hours, four hospitals had been
erased.

The commandant returned without bread, but Chef Kwiecinski said he would make soup from what was left of the
horses.

We were nauseated with the stench of decomposing bodies.
Thousands of dead bodies were lying under debris or in their
homes, and thousands of Germans were lying unburied in the
outskirts.

We were almost suffocated with the smoke. The city was
in flames, and the wind began to blow.

The ministry office opposite us was on fire. The whole
street, where fire had raged once before only to be extin-

guished by the hailstone storm, was aflame, and the wind carried the burning fragments to our side of the street.

We had to direct almost all our resources to fighting the fire. We had only the operaing theater working, and wounded were being continually brought in. Except for Dr. Szymanski, who was not young—he would be on call in Maltanski in case of emergency—all the doctors were needed to fight the fire. We went through the wards and informed the wounded of the situation, and asked for their help; we asked them, that is, to see that no panic arose and to help the nurse. There would be only one nurse in the ward, as we needed the others to help protect Maltanski from the fire.

The commandant and the sentries, the attendants, stretcher-bearers, doctors, nurses, secretaries, and all other available hands were breaking down the walls of the house on our left to arrest the fire.

On the right of Maltanski was a building in course of construction, which was surrounded by wooden scaffolding. Burning fragments were falling on this building. If it took fire, our hospital would be lost. That area was the sector I was defending. Though it required no physical force, it did require constant vigilance. Messenger boys were on all floors of the scaffolding, stamping out sparks and pushing off the bigger burning fragments. We had no water.

A German pilot flew over us at his leisure, dropping incendiary bombs. I saw eight such bombs fall on the roof of Maltanski. Good God! The hospital will be burned! I was standing on the roof of the neighboring construction. Could I get down in time? Had anyone downstairs seen the bombs? The noise of explosions was so loud that if I called no one would hear me. I managed to get down, though moving up or down on a scaffolding is not easy—there was no staircase.

The chef had seen the bombs from the kitchen window. He had grabbed a meat-chopper, called his staff, and was already on the roof. By the time I had gotten down, the fires were out.

Chef Kwiecinski then returned to preparing the soup for dinner, limping proudly because he had kicked a bomb down from the roof and had trampled out the incipient fires. Maltanski was saved for the time being.

When the soup was ready, the boys ran down in turn to have a bowl. I had no one to relieve me, and could not leave my post on the scaffolding. Chef Kwiecinski, however, remembered, and John, the messenger, brought soup up for me. To climb five floors of scaffolding with a bowl of soup is quite an achievement for anyone. Perhaps John's bicycle rides on the glass roof of the bank had prepared him for the equilibristic performance.

In the afternoon the fire reached the street behind our garden. Teams had to be divided. The commandant remained in the front, and Dr. Fenski took charge of fighting the new danger, taking with him doctors, nurses, and stretcher-bearers. Chef Kwiecinski joined him with his staff. The new fires behind the hospital affected my sector. In the back, touching our garden, was a synagogue, which, being under repair, was also surrounded by scaffolding. My task and the boys' was now to prevent it from catching fire from burning debris carried by the wind.

The new situation required that half of the messengers' group be sent to the scaffolding around the synagogue. That weakened the morale of the boys, for they were no longer together in a single group. A sense of defeat began to creep up on us, and I do not know of a more corrosive process. The terrific bombing and artillery fire were a background to our fight against the wall of flames.

When night came, our general situation was the same, but in my sector it had worsened. In the daytime every boy could see me at the top of the new construction, and could feel that he would be given help when he needed it. In reality, I could be of little help when up there to the boys on the scaffolding of the synagogue. But still each one could see me and I could see each of them; we were a unit. When night came, none of them knew where I was until I, on my constant rounds, came to ask how he was doing. I was tired too—I was not used to climbing up and down scaffoldings.

We knew that if any one sector failed to hold out, Maltanski would be lost. Every hour on the hour, the commandant, Dr. Fenski, and I met in the hall to discuss whether we could hold out an hour longer.

About three o'clock in the morning the wind became a tempest. The artillery fire was more deadly than ever. The boys had been on the scaffolding for fourteen hours; for days they had been receiving little food, and all they had had in the past twenty-four hours was a bowl of soup in the early afternoon. They were so faint and weak that they could hardly stand. I realized that my sector would not be able to hold out for more than an hour.

Maltanski was singing: "Holy God, great and powerful, great and eternal, have mercy on us." We could hear the hymn on the scaffolding.

It was apparent that we must begin evacuating the wounded out to the garden. It was now our turn to become a homeless hospital. We could not hope for a miracle every time, and I hardly dared to expect one more, for humanly speaking there seemed to be no escape.

I left the scaffolding to meet with the commandant and Dr. Fenski in the hospital. The noise of explosions was so loud that we had to shout to each other. We did not hear an explosion that took place in the adjoining ward (ward number one), but the door to it suddenly burst open, and we heard screams of "Help!" A shell had passed through the window of the second floor, gone through to ward number one, on the first floor, and burst under the bed of a wounded lieutenant. He and eight other patients were killed, but a young nurse,

Countess Renata Ostrowski, who was near the bed under which the shell exploded, was only thrown to the opposite side of the ward, her coat torn.

When we rushed to the ward, seconds after the explosion, that young nurse was already at work. She remained on duty till morning.

I went out again to in front of the hospital. The wind had changed direction. The miracle had taken place. Once more Maltanski was saved.

Wednesday, September 27, 1939

We worked from daybreak on to clear ward number one, in the hope that we would have it ready for use before evening.

The body of the lieutenant under whose bed the shell had been exploded had been blown into pieces, and the pieces had been thrown everywhere—on the walls, on the ceiling. Both his legs had just been amputated, and he had been laid on a bed in the middle of the ward. The nurse, having no place to put a chair for herself, had sat on the floor by the bed to wait till he should wake up; that was why she had escaped death, although she was within three feet of the shell. The girl was lucky; on the sixteenth she had similarly escaped when ward number five had been bombed.

The beds in ward number one were jammed together, and it was difficult to entangle the heap of torn pillows and mattresses. The crater in the floor was ten feet deep and fifteen feet in diameter. We had to fill it and find planks to improvise a floor. By afternoon the ward was ready, except that it had no beds. We needed its floor space badly, as some wounded were lying on the sidewalk.

At two o'clock, suddenly—silence . . .

The planes were not seen any more; the artillery fire ceased. Our hearts stopped for a moment. What did it mean?

It was a twenty-four hour armistice to permit burial of the dead.

Late that afternoon we received gas masks from headquarters and distributed them to the wounded and the staff. Apparently we were threatened with poison gas—but we would worry about that later. What everyone was looking forward to was a night's sleep. The wounded in the wards told us that they would take care of themselves that night as they had done the day before, to let the nursing staff rest.

I made rounds until one o'clock in the morning, when Josette took over.

At midnight I was with Lieutenant Ozelski when he died. In civilian life he had been a post-office clerk in a small country town. In the battle of Kutno, about 100 miles from Warsaw, he was wounded in the arm by an explosive bullet. To avoid being taken prisoner by the Germans, he had started out for Warsaw on foot. That part of the country was already occupied by the Germans, and for days he had hidden in the daytime and walked at night, without food and without his wound being treated. He had sneaked into Warsaw through the enemy lines, and a cart had picked him up. When he was brought to us his temperature was very high, he was almost delirious, and he was so ill that there was no possibility of saving his life. But, as he wished, he had not been taken prisoner by the Germans.

If death could be beautiful, most beautiful was the death of Lieutenant Ozelski. In his delirium he believed he was still among his men, and he began to speak to them about Poland, the land of our fathers—about the cause for which they were fighting, about the duty of every human being to fulfill himself to his capacity, about how much greatness and beauty there was in Poland. And he reminded them that we were all fighting for the survival of the things that were most precious to us. He spoke so calmly that a hush of reverence fell over the ward. To conclude his message, the lieutenant told his men that they should now sing the national anthem; in the stillness of the ward one could almost hear it.

Lieutenant Ozelski's face was very calm; he seemed to be listening to the anthem. But his wide-open eyes were already looking into eternity.

Thursday, September 28, 1939

At nine in the morning, the commandants of all hospitals were called to headquarters.

I went to the Red Cross early to find out whether we would receive any bread that day. As I could not get an answer then, I went to headquarters at ten o'clock—also to pick up the commandant. Before I could inquire whether the meeting was over, I saw an officer coming down the staircase dancing and singing—"Capitulation! Capitulation!" Then he drew his revolver and shot himself.

Dazed, I went out, not knowing where to go. I could not return just now to Maltanski to face my people. My apartment house had been burned. I wandered for a few hours, not seeing, not hearing, not feeling. Suddenly I looked up; I was in front of Maltanski. The news of our capitulation was already known, and it had also been heard that Poland was to to be divided between Germany and the Soviet Union, with the Vistula as the demarcation line.

The commandant returned from headquarters. What a change a few hours can make in a man! He looked many

years older. Trying to appear calm, in a voice broken and
halting, he gave us the official news:

"I come from headquarters. Since nine o'clock the talks
have been about the conditions of capitulation. We have no
more ammunition. The armistice will last till two P.M. From
two till five P.M. we will be given time to complete the nego-
tiations. The barricades are to be removed and the army is to
be withdrawn from their positions to the center of the city.

"Whether the officers only, or the troops as well, will be
taken to concentration camps is not yet known. Those who
feel strong enough should remain at their posts. How the Germans will act toward the Red Cross and the Sovereign Order
of the Knights of Malta Corps remains to be seen.

"There is still time before three P.M. to cross the Vistula to
the Praga district. To whom that part of Warsaw will belong
is not yet known. It is possible that Praga will be turned over
to the Soviet Army.

"After 5 P.M. no one will be allowed to go out into the
streets; what our destiny will be in the evening is unknown.

"We shall get food for three days, after which civilian
patients must be taken from Maltanski to the regular hospitals.
The soldiers will remain here.

"All the news we trusted about rescue is untrue—no one is
coming to help us. Not a shot has been fired in our defense.
Now we are waiting to see what the Germans will decide to
do with us."

We sat in silence—Mrs. Glinski, Senator Szymanski, Stas,
Monsignor Dobiecki, Josette, and I. It was the first time since
Dominik and Roman had been killed that the executive council
met. It began to dawn upon me that they would never return.

But there was no room for personal feelings; we had a
responsibility to help our staff discharge their duties to the
wounded. We decided to talk separately with each service

and then to be available for individual consultations. The commandant was to go to another meeting at headquarters before five P.M. After his return we were to meet again.

When I met with the nursing staff, I reported the official communiques and then asked them to make a still greater effort than before, because our task was heavier that day than at any other time. They had been courageous when the bombs were falling and now they had to be courageous when the world we believed in was crumbling. The first stage of the war was over. But the war itself was not over, and we had to work with set teeth in preparation for the freedom of Poland, if it took months, years, or a lifetime.

There were practical matters that we had to consider. The civilian wounded were to be taken out of our hospital, and the wounded from our military hospital number two were to be moved in. We would discharge any patient who could be cared for outside the hospital before we had to submit the list of patients to the enemy, because from that moment on patients would be considered prisoners of war.

We would have a normal population of wounded; reduction of staff was imminent. W easked everyone to let us know whether he or she had a home to go to, because that would be our criterion in the reduction of personnel.

The commandant returned from headquarters, but he had nothing new to add.

Our military command had compiled a list of persons to be decorated with the Military Cross. Maltanski was cited as a unit, and the names of ninety-six members of our staff were also on the list individually.

In the evening I had to go downtown. Jacek Goldman drove me. While we were driving along the avenue that runs across the city I could look around for the first time. We drove by five miles of smoldering, gutted houses. I understood the wisdom and charity of the orders that no one was to be in the street after five o'clock. There was our army, marching, disarmed, and silent. Goldman was sobbing, Goldman, who was the man without fear. Where was our mask of warriors? I did not cry, because tears would not come. Without doing my errand, I returned to Maltanski.

Night came. The fires were dying out in clouds of dirty smoke. Many shots were heard all through the night. Who was shooting at whom?

I went through the hospital. For what, I wondered, had we saved those patients? For humiliation? For concentration camps? For slavery?

A young soldier called to me: "I have no legs, but still I am sure that one day, even if I cannot have artificial legs, I can go on a cart to fight. And fight I will!" Yes, I thought, we all would fight, only now it would be more difficult.

In the kitchen all the drivers, sentries, and stretcher-bearers were sitting in silence, some of them weeping. "What shall I do with the champagne you brought for our liberation?" asked Chef Kwiecinski, bitter and distressed. Yes, what should we do? All the champagne in the world could not stop something that hurts so terribly inside. Everything was so unimportant.

"In France," said a sentry, "a Polish army has been formed. We shall go on foot to join it, and fight; we shall defend them, their country, their homes. Do you think they will help us too, after they have victory?" A seminarian, one of the stretcher-bearers got up. "Why?" he said, "Why? Can you tell us why?" "Yes," I said, "because of five words on our Polish flag, 'For our freedom and yours'. That's why."

All the time we heard singing, as we did in our darkest hours, one ward taking up the hymn from the other, so that it went on through the night:

O God, Who throughout the centuries,
Surrounded Poland with the luster of power and glory,
Shielding her with Thy protection
Against the misfortunes which oppressed her,
Before Thine altar we bring our supplications.
O, Lord, deign to bless and give our Fatherland her
Freedom once more.

And so that night passed.

Friday, September 29, and Saturday, September 30, 1939

Those two days were not only full of distress; they were
ugly. People crawled out of shelters, looked around and realized that their way of life, whatever it had been, was over.
People understood that their integrity as human beings would
be crushed. The integrity of a human being rests on the right
to choose. In the totalitarian way of life there is no room for
choice. People did not need to be sophisticated to realize that
someone else would now make decisions for them, that they
would be someone else's property, that someone else would
decide whether they would live and what they would become.
Since the integrity of a human being rests on the right to
choose, to surrender it, is to surrender what one is.

That was Warsaw: miles of streets with smoldering or
burned out houses, some of them standing like empty shells,
others crumbled into heaps of rubble. There was no means of
communication other than by foot. There was no light, no
water, no food, and no law. For what kind of life could a
human being take responsibility? Where could one begin?
How? On what premise? The principles in which we believed,
on which we had based our lives, and which we wanted to

preserve, had been violated and the evidence was before our eyes.

Masses of people crawled out of shelters, many bewildered by the reality they faced. Distressed by hunger, loss, and uncertainty, people took refuge in crowds. In no time at all the crowds became mobs. A mob can do anything, can give way to any feeling, because in a mob people do not feel individually responsible.

In its hour of capitulation, Warsaw was in disgrace. Mobs were growing in size and violence. Looting, rape, and murder were rife.

There were oases in Warsaw where thinking and planning were intense. One of those places was Maltanski. Many people came to exchange thoughts and news and whatever gossip they had heard, and to inquire about relatives.

The commandant—my brother Stas—and I were glad that we had not insisted that our sister leave Warsaw for the "safety" of the eastern part of Poland. She would have been swallowed into the Soviet Union a few hours after the Red Army had crossed the Polish frontier. Her husband, who was in the Army of Poznan, was missing. The Army of Poznan had been massacred in its attempt to break into Warsaw on the twentieth. Our brother Andrew was also missing. All we knew was that his regiment had been in the eastern part of Poland. Perhaps he had been taken prisoner. We learned that prisoners of war were being shipped into Russia, officers and men in different directions.[14]

Our concern was over how the Germans and the Russians would partition our country. If the Vistula was to be the dividing line, Warsaw would be divided between the two.

We wondered how long the friendship between Germany and Russia would last, and which would attack the other first. At that time the Russians were less than 300 miles from Berlin; the Germans were 1000 miles from Moscow.

Zwerdling, my driver, came to cheer me up. He said that I should not be worried about the possibility of the Russians' taking over Warsaw. He told me that he had such good connections that he would arrange for a guard of honor to be at my door. He realized, he added, that he was a hero. Since a hero should have money, he said he would leave and go into business, but that he would be a guest at Maltanski as often as he could.[15]

We were aware that we would have to submit a list of the names of our wounded soldiers and of our staff to the enemy. We felt that if a wounded man could avoid being on that list he should do so, and we were trying to have as many leave Maltanski as was possible. The medical staff was busy helping the wounded to leave.

As we did not trust that the Geneva Convention would be respected, we preferred to handle the fate of the Jewish members of our staff ourselves. Monsignor Dobiecki had a stack of personal documents belonging to people who had been killed. We felt that those people would not mind if we used their papers to help countrymen of Jewish descent. It was a laborious job to match resemblances, ages, and sex. We made this service available to all who desired it, regardless of whether they were going to stay with us or preferred to leave.

When I told Zwerdling about it, he said that he had already had things figured out; there would be a great demand for passports, and therefore he would manufacture them. He would rather have a new name of his own choice on a new passport, than someone else's name, which he might not like, he said. He added that I had not had an opportunity to acquaint myself with all his talents.

Sad news came from the west. In the region of Poznan, the Germans were publicly executing numbers of people as a preventive measure and as a warning. In the town of Kostrzyn, which had been the county seat where my sister had lived before Poland was attacked, the Germans had picked at random sixteen representatives of different professions and trades for execution; then they had rounded up the whole population—men, women, and children—and forced them to watch the execution of the sixteen. One of the sixteen had been Count Jan Szoldrski, the father of one of our patients.

From the eastern part of Poland the news was alarming. The populations of whole villages were being rounded up and deported to Siberia. Prince Janusz Radziwill had been deported to the Soviet Union, together with his wife, daughter-in-law, and grandchildren.

There was a constant stream of people coming to Maltanski for comfort. People needed understanding and support more than when the fighting had been going on. They wished to reassure themselves that human beings could retain their integrity when everything was crumbling around them.

During the siege only one category of people had been seen on the streets of Warsaw: people bound together by one purpose, people who had developed in themselves the highest values of humanity and who—some with surprise—had discovered that they possessed values of which they had been unaware before the siege.

During the siege, greed, selfishness, cowardliness, simple indecision, and weakness had been hidden underground in cellars and in any place wheer a creature could tuck himself away for safety. Now those creatures were out, and we, the defenders of Warsaw, were looking at them as if they were cockroaches, as if they were not human beings who now had to face the same losses and uncertainties as we did. The gap between us had become so wide that it was impossible for many a weak, frightened creature to follow our way of thinking. And what did we do to help them?

Perhaps in this hour of trial we had overlooked the factor most important in human life—to be accepted, to belong, to be someone who is respected and wanted. Our leadership had not yet gained vision enough to be helpful to people who were as distressed as we were. At that time no one knew where to turn for assistance or where to begin. No one could know what the invaders had in store for him.

Our understanding was limited; we could not feel our compassion for the weak, for the cowardly. We lacked an important dimension.

What a shame that the leader of a mob could provide what we had failed to do—acceptance and understanding—which people needed so badly. Can one be surprised that the mobs increased, that people from all walks of life followed the mobs rather than following us, who at that time were inaccessible, and who had withheld from them the acceptance and leadership they most needed in a time of disintegration?

Thomas, a young seminarian, returned from an afternoon in the city in such distress that we were afraid of what he might do to himself. Thomas had been sheltered all his life. From under the wings of his mother he had gone directly to a seminary to train for the priesthood, and had been there only a few months when Germany attacked. He had then come with a group of seminarians to Maltanski to work as a stretcher-bearer.

He sobbed out his story. That afternoon's excursion into the city had been his first independent action; he had never before learned how to handle himself outside of a cage. He had walked through the city, distressed by the destruction he saw and horrified at the expression on the faces of the people. He had found himself moving with a crowd. At first he had been curious and repelled. But before he knew it, he had become one of the mob, and it had made him feel more powerful than he had ever felt before. He had felt happy and carefree. Nothing had mattered in this world but the present. The gates to a factory had burst open, and the mob had poured into the yard. What factory it had been did not matter; now it was his. From the windows of an upper story persons who had pushed themselves inside had begun to throw out cartons of cigarettes and boxes of cigars. People in the yard were pushing and trampling on one another to catch whatever they could. Thomas was tall and strong; he could stretch his arms and push anyone aside. He had caught a box of cigars and tucked it under his coat.

The mob had moved on. Those who had been trampled had been left behind, but no one had cared. Thomas had seen them with his eyes, but not with his feelings. He had felt happy—he had seen too much unhappiness in the past few weeks. Nothing could spoil his happiness now.

The mob had broken into a bakery, where loaves of bread stood on shelves. "You wanted to have big business," shouted the leader to the baker. "Well, you have big business; you have customers." Loaves of bread were grabbed; loaves of bread were thrown over heads to outstretched hands, and torn from the hands of one person by another. What had it mattered to Thomas? He had tucked a whole loaf, still hot under his coat. It was more bread than he had seen in weeks. The mob had moved on again. Thomas by that time had been near the leader; he had felt great and powerful. They had come upon a small store, which had escaped destruction. The storekeeper stood at the door. "Let us see what he has for us," the leader said, and the mob had followed him. "Oh, no, you will not come in here, except over my dead body," shouted the storekeeper and blocked the entrance. "Ooooh, yes!" said the leader, and his fist felled the man. He stepped on the man's chest and entered the store; the mob followed.

Thomas had stood paralyzed with horror. He had snapped out of the mob's hypnotic grip. A woman stood wailing that she had missed the robbing of the bakery. Thomas pushed his loaf into her hands, threw his box of cigars as far as he could, and began to run. No matter how fast he ran, no matter in which direction, before his eyees was the body of the unconscious storekeeper, with those convulsive twitches that he had seen many times in wounded men who were beyond assistance —a man who had done nothing to him, who only wanted to protect what was his. When he could run no more, he had come back to Maltanski.

Some members of the staff came to the commandant and asked him to order the boy punished; if he were punished, they said, he would not feel such distress. The commandant had been authorized by martial law to order punishment up to twenty-five lashes.

Thomas was haggard when he came to the office. He said that he would take fifty lashes, that he would take 100; that he deserved them. He wanted to be punished, painfully, severely, and quickly.

The commandant told Thomas that he would not order even a single lash, for if he did he would have to share with Thomas the responsibility for the deed. Instead of that, he said, Thomas would have to take full responsibility himself. He went on to say that a boy becomes a man at a price. Perhaps taking responsibility for his afternoon's actions was the price Thomas would pay for becoming a man. The day's experience had shown how easy it was to change from a hero to a thief and an accomplice in murder.

One needed more strength in those two days than at any other time during the siege. People were dazed. Everyone was in some way off balance.

We had received an order from headquarters to send all civilian wounded to civilian hospitals, because after October first, we were to become a prisoner-of-war camp, and would receive food rations only for the military. At that time we had enough bread for only one day.

We had few civilians, by now, among the wounded in Maltanski, but we felt responsible for the welfare of those in our civilian annex. As most of our wounded in the annex were Jewish, we needed to plan with someone who represented the Jewish community, and arranged for a meeting with a rabbi. The commandant and I went to meet him in the annex and we discussed problems of shelter, food, and medical care.

Some of the wounded could not be moved without danger to their lives. Some could be moved, but there was no adequate means of transportation. Also, there was little room for them in civilian hospitals.

There is a Polish proverb that says that on the granite rock of principles roses do not bloom. We had our orders, but we did not know how to execute them, and therefore we decided that we would wait for the time being, until we received instructions on how to follow them. We would take this chance.

We decided to leave the Jewish wounded where they were. No one could prevent us from giving them medical care; and the rabbi would assume responsibility for feeding them.

We were notified that the next day, October 1, the German Army would enter the city.

That was our last evening before becoming prisoners of war. We met in the office—the commandant, Senator Szymanski, Monsignor Dobiecki, Mrs. Glinski, Josette, and I. We went over our obligations to the wounded and to the staff, to see whether we had overlooked something. We felt that everything possible had been done. We were tired, extremely tired. There was no more use for the mask of warriors. The mask of warriors, which each of us had assumed at first, was a mask modeled on poetry, or tradition, or heroic stories; on recruitment posters, on parades, and on songs. Those patterns no longer fitted our reality; they never had. The night was dark; the fires were dying out. Stray shots were heard all over the city.

There is no glory in capitulation.

Maltanski was quiet. We could sleep that night.

On the first day of October the German Army entered Warsaw. But it was not the same army that had been attacking us. A parade army was brought for this occasion. It was designed in characteristic German fashion to be an impressive pageant, with full military splendor, and of course, with music and drums. Every soldier was shaved and groomed, and wore a new uniform. The whole day they marched around the city with tommy-guns pointed every few feet at the silent people. But the parade was far from being a triumph. In every eye the Germans could have read that which has followed them ever since. . . . But the eyes of those armed German soldiers did not dare to look at us—disarmed.

NOTES

1. Marta Korwin is the name which the author assumed in May 1940, when escaping from Poland.

2. The Sovereign Order of the Knights of Malta came into being at the time of Crusades, in the eleventh century, and was first known as the Order of St. John of Jerusalem. Its original concern was founding hospitals for pilgrims to the Holy Land.

As the centuries passed it became a great military order, but never ceased to serve the sick and the poor.

To be admitted to the Order as a Knight of Honor and Devotion one must prove that his "sixteen quarters" belong to the nobility, and that he is of desirable character.

There are several other degrees of knighthood in the Order for which the requirements are less strict.

3. Stanislaw Count Korwin-Milewski-Lipkowski, Knight of Honor and Devotion.

4. Jan Count Kwilecki, Knight of Honor and Devotion.

5. The buses with the gold started northeast in the direction of Pinsk. As they went, the drivers heard their location given to German planes. To escape attack, the drivers therefore changed their direction and went south, crossed the Romanian border, drove to Constanta on the Black Sea, and loaded their cargo on a British merchant ship. Their moves were so unpredictable that the gold was on the ship before anyone could stop them. Romanian authorities notified the captain that the ship would be sunk if she moved. But at dusk the ship left Constanta and reached Istanbul next morning. It was not possible to go through the Dardanelles without clearance, and clearance had not been granted. Moreover, information reached the Polish Ambassador in Istanbul that a German ship

planned to collide with the "gold ship" in the night and sink her. The ship sailed in the evening as if about to defy orders and risk the Dardanelles. But she unexpectedly changed her direction and reached the Asiatic side of the Sea of Marmara. The gold was unloaded onto a train and was moved by land to Izmir, where the British Navy, from a base in Alexandria, could give it protection. Then it was loaded on a ship again and moved to safety.

6. The course, soon interrupted, was resumed after the siege. Diplomas were awarded early in 1940, by Prince Janusz Radziwill when he returned to Warsaw after being released from a prison in the Soviet Union.

7. Stephan Count Zyberg-Plater undertook to photograph, for documentary purposes, what was happening during the siege of Warsaw. Later he carried out this activity as his contribution to the underground. Most of the photographs of German atrocities, which were smuggled out of Poland and supplied the free world with evidence of what was really going on under the Nazi occupation, were taken by him.

During the occupation the Germans tried to catch red-handed the person who was taking the photographs that were appearing in the free world, especially in the United States. Many times the Germans raided Stephan's apartment and searched the studio, but they never found anything, as the underground always removed the evidence quickly. Once, however, they almost got him. Stephan was vulnerable for the few hours it took to develop the negatives and make prints. The Gestapo came to his home, took him and his wife to the studio, and began a thorough search. But they did not pay any attention to the maid, whom they left at her work in the kitchen. The negatives at that time had already been removed from his home, but the prints were floating in the bathtub. The maid slipped into the bathroom, stuck the dripping prints inside her clothes, and left unnoticed, by the back door. She hid for hours on the roof, with the temperature below zero, until she was certain the danger was over. For the next two years Stephan was lucky. But in 1943 he was arrested, and imprisoned for some time in Auschwitz concentration camp, where he finally was executed.

8. Many of the donors of beds had nothing left after the siege, and inquired whether we could keep our commitments. We were able to purchase some beds in small towns that were not entirely destroyed and we delivered them to the people who had given their beds to us when we needed them most. We made good our pledges even in cases in which the claimant could not produce a receipt or any other proof of donation.

9. Maltanski Hospital continued its work until 1944, when the Germans burned it down during the Warsaw Insurrection. The German Army removed their own wounded from the building, poured gasoline under the beds, and then burned the hospital and the patients. My brother Stas tried to stop them, but was shot and seriously wounded. Someone dragged him out of the holocaust.

10. After the capitulation of Warsaw, President Starzynski was taken away by the Germans. No news was ever heard of him.

11. Andrew Pachulski remained with the hospital when it became a prisoner-of-war camp. While performing his duties there as a messenger, he was seized by the Germans and executed.

12. After the capitulation, there were no Polish military authorities; therefore, persons who had been sentenced by court-martial were released.

13. This case had a happy ending. After weeks of suffering he left Maltanski able to use both arms; one elbow was stiff— this we hoped to correct later. Moreover, when he left, he was engaged to the nurse who had been caring for him.

14. Soldiers up to the rank of sergeant were deported to Siberia. Officers were taken to various camps. In March 1940, about 11,000 were executed in the forests of Katyn.

15. Jacob Zwerdling started several businesses, including the manufacture of passports. A few weeks after he left Maltanski he changed his name to Joseph Pawlowicz, M.D., and own plant to everyone in Maltanski. He bought and sold exhibited a passport with his new name manufactured in his diamonds, gold, and currency. He forged German marks, which he then sold to German soldiers at half price. However, he kept his own capital in gold. He bought stolen gasoline from German soldiers and sold it to anyone who could not obtain gasoline officially.

Maltanski was buying gasoline from Zwerdling because we needed it for underground activities and obviously did not wish to account to the Germans for it, as we had to for gasoline purchased officially. I was in charge of gasoline, and kept it in the vaults of the bank where we used to have the operating theater. Once he cheated me by a few gallons. I did not expect that, was greatly shocked, and told him what I thought of it. Zwerdling's reply was disarming. "I could not help it when I had the opportunity," he said, "but I am a gentleman and I will make up for it." Accordingly, Zwerdling gave the hospital a 100-gallon drum of gasoline, 1,000 zlotys ($200) for medical supplies, and twelve passports with all necessary visas. That was not all; I received from him a five-foot bush of white lilac in bloom. Where he got it from—in December— was a mystery.

Every few weeks Zwerdling came to Maltanski to ask us to keep a heavy parcel safely for him. One day he asked for the return of his deposit, which he displayed to us and which appeared to contain more than 20,000 gold coins. He said he was paying the Gestapo as part of some big transaction, after which he would buy a plane and fly to France, as there was no life outside the south of France. We tried to discourage him from going to the wolf's den with that golden fleece. But so great was Zwerdling's need to show off, to gamble, to defy authority, that he did not listen to us. The Gestapo, as we expected, did not turn out to be a safe business partner; Zwerdling disappeared. Many days later we received a note from him asking us to send him a food parcel, in prison. The fortune he had made in four months was gone. Poor Zwerdling would have to start all over again. As I escaped from Poland soon afterwards, however, I do not know the epilogue to Zwerdling's adventures.